The French Art of Not Giving a Sh*t

The French Art *of Not* Giving a Sh*t

FABRICE MIDAL

Translated by Ian Monk

hachette
BOOKS

NEW YORK   BOSTON

Hachette Books
Hachette Book Group
1290 Avenue of the Americas
New York, NY 10104
hachettebooks.com
twitter.com/hachettebooks

Scripture quotations taken from the 21st Century King James Version®, copyright © 1994. Used by permission of Deuel Enterprises, Inc., Gary, SD 57237. All rights reserved. (KJ21)

Permissions

Excerpt from René Char, *Les Matinaux* © Editions Gallimard, Paris, 1950.

Excerpt from Henri Michaux, *Poteaux d'angle* © Editions Gallimard, Paris, 1981.

Excerpt from Georges Braque, *Le Jour et la Nuit*. Cahier 1917–1952 © Editions Gallimard, Paris, 1952

Excerpt from *The Letters of Emily Dickinson*, edited by Thomas H. Johnson, Associate Editor, Theodora Ward, Cambridge, Mass.: The Belknap Press of Harvard University Press, Copyright © 1958 by the President and Fellows of Harvard College. Copyright © renewed 1986 by the President and Fellows of Harvard College. Copyright © 1914, 1924, 1932, 1942 by Martha Dickinson Bianchi. Copyright © 1952 by Alfred Leete Hampson. Copyright © 1960 by Mary L. Hampson.

Excerpt from *Sonnets to Orpheus* by Rainer Marie Rilke. Translation and Introduction © 1987 by David Young. Published by Wesleyan University Press. Used by permission.

Excerpts from *The Little Prince* by Antoine de Saint Exupery. Copyright © 1943 by Houghton Mifflin Harcourt Publishing Company, renewed 1972 by Consuelo de Saint Exupery, English translation copyright ©2000 by Richard Howard. Reprinted by permission of Houghton Mifflin Harcourt Publishing Company. All rights reserved.

Originally published as *Foutez-Vous La Paix! ET Commencez á Vivre* by Editions Flammarion/Versilio in France in 2017.

First U.S. edition: December 2017

Hachette Books is a division of Hachette Book Group, Inc.

The Hachette Books name and logo are trademarks of Hachette Book Group, Inc.

The publisher is not responsible for websites (or their content) that are not owned by the publisher.

LCCN: 2017952442
ISBNs: 978-0-316-47821-2 (hardcover), 978-0-316-47823-6 (ebook)

Printed in the United States of America

LSC-C

10 9 8 7 6 5 4 3 2 1

Contents

Introduction   *ix*

Chapter One: *Stop Meditating*   *1*

Chapter Two: *Stop Obeying*   *11*

Chapter Three: *Stop Being Wise*   *23*

Chapter Four: *Stop Being Calm*   *34*

Chapter Five: *Stop Holding Yourself Back*   *46*

Chapter Six: *Stop Being Passive*   *52*

Chapter Seven: *Stop Being Conscious*   *59*

Chapter Eight: *Stop Wanting to Be Perfect*   *66*

Chapter Nine: *Stop Trying to Understand Everything*   *77*

Contents

Chapter Ten: *Stop Rationalizing*   84

Chapter Eleven: *Stop Comparing*   89

Chapter Twelve: *Stop Being Ashamed*   98

Chapter Thirteen: *Stop Tormenting Yourself*   105

Chapter Fourteen: *Stop Wanting to Love*   116

Chapter Fifteen: *Stop Disciplining Your Kids*   119

Conclusion   126

Appendix   133

Notes   143

Further Reading   155

Acknowledgments   159

The French Art of Not
Giving a Sh*t

INTRODUCTION

I have been hosting conferences and seminars in schools, businesses, and hospitals for many years now, and I always inevitably come away with the same conclusion: We spend all day tormenting ourselves.

We torment ourselves into adopting norms, rules, and models that don't necessarily work for us. We torment ourselves because we want to do better, but we feel as if we never actually achieve the best result. We torment ourselves because we're sure that other people know how to do better than us. We often torment ourselves even without anything being asked of us.

We are caught up in frenetic activity that completely blinds us. Gripped by the need to do, we no longer see that in reality we're doing nothing; after getting all worked up, we forget what's truly important. We forget how to live.

So, it's time to stop giving a shit! My experience has taught me that there is no better way to rediscover our potential and the forgotten possibilities that lie within us. Just stop! It's time to break free from unnecessary protocols and procedures, to take a leave from self-imposed stresses. And when you do, you will discover a well of energy enabling you to go that extra mile.

You don't need to escape to the top of a mountain or the depths of a cave to think: Stay right where you are and stop forcing yourself to think so hard. Give yourself a break; it's the best way to get by in a world full of suffering, misery, and inhumanity. We need to make a change now. You can start today, by not giving a shit...

—Fabrice Midal

I

STOP MEDITATING

Do nothing

Never ask your way from someone who knows it. You might fail to get lost.
—Rabbi Nachman of Bretslov[1]

Do I meditate? This is something I occasionally think about when I see the avalanche of books and conferences that all exhort us to practice meditation, endeavor to teach us its techniques, and glibly reel off its benefits.

Do I meditate? No, not as such. I never force myself to do so, and when I don't feel like meditating, I do something else.

I don't use a specific technique, nor do I rely on any set of instructions. I meditate to free myself from all forms of command.

And my aim is not to become wise, or calm, or patient. I have no aim, no objective, not even the idea of starting or finishing the day in any particular state of mind.

I've been meditating for more than twenty-five years, and I have been teaching the practice for almost fifteen, but I have no techniques to hand over or empty promises to make. When I started teaching, many people actually predicted that I would fail. What could I possibly teach when the groundwork for my practice is that meditation is unproductive, that it doesn't make you more efficient, it doesn't make you wiser, and that, deep down, it has no "purpose," in the common sense of the term? But in fact, it's precisely *because* meditation frees us from being enslaved to the modern demands of usefulness and profitability that we are lucky it exists.

Over the years, I've seen this obsession with performance turn toxic in the world around me. Profitability and usefulness have become the world's mantra...and meditation is in no way exempt. I have witnessed countless new manuals and exercises guaranteeing results after ten or twenty sessions of mindful meditation, almost to the point of prescribing a proper dosage. We are told that meditation should be used in companies to improve profitability, in schools to heighten students' concentration and efficacy, and at home to feel less stressed.

I see beginner meditators confused, then disgusted, because their apprenticeship has failed: They haven't been transformed, nor do they even feel less stressed. Presumably, they tell me, they haven't concentrated hard enough, or they have failed to detach themselves from their thoughts. They've been distracted, they haven't been sitting properly—or maybe their chosen technique, which was in fact quite difficult, wasn't the right one for them. In fact, they've worked themselves up to a state of nervous anticipation, as if they were about to take an oral exam. But as we all know, the tenser you are, the more you focus on the need to succeed, the greater the risk of showing up with a knotted throat and sweaty hands. You experience more fear than enjoyment, and thus you have a higher chance of failing.

This type of meditation is not mine. Meditation, as I see it, is not a technique or an exercise, and there's nothing mysterious about it: It is an art of living. The art of not giving a shit. I prescribe nothing, I guarantee nothing, I provide no tricks or tips. I don't suggest you observe your thoughts as they pass by without lingering over them, like clouds that end up fading away. This kind of technique is not inherently *wrong*, but in practice it quickly turns out to be tedious and downright boring. And when you're bored, you're no longer alive. I have no desire to torture myself over some idea that I need to meditate. I'm more interested in the intelligence and humanity of those around me. I know that what I have to say will raise some eyebrows, but I deeply believe it's true.

In the end, you meditate only when you *stop trying* to meditate: when you rid yourself of the absolute need to achieve, to accomplish, to meet a goal, and thus to be anxious about failing. Of course, I have my moments when I'm uptight; but ordering myself to relax is the best way to get even *more* uptight. And to torture myself. I don't even have to wait for someone to tell me to relax in order to feel stressed, because I'm very good at torturing myself on my own. Like most people, I tend to want to do things well. So well that I put extreme pressure on myself. I set challenges and then panic about not being able to live up to them. Yet I know from experience that when I simply observe that I'm uptight, and I sincerely allow myself to continue to be so—in other words, when I don't give a shit about being uptight—then funnily enough, I usually end up relaxing very quickly.

Daring to give yourself a break—which is at once so simple and so complicated—and having the audacity to actually not give a shit, *that* is what I call meditation.

I remember how my grandparents used to spend ages silently staring at a fire smoldering in the fireplace. As Communists, they had distanced themselves from religion and spirituality. They were far from being mystics and had never heard of meditation, but their evenings in front of the fire were as close as you can get to what I call meditation. For them, it was a form of mental hygiene. An act that was natural, banal, but indispensable. As natural and banal as walking, moving, getting tired, or doing what we call exercise—which now involves expert advice, machines, instructions, and devices used to measure our performance, which we then use to compare ourselves with others. Our great-grandparents didn't need to go for a run to stay fit.

I was fourteen when I first heard about the practice of meditation, which at the time was virtually unknown. It intrigued me, but I was afraid that I'd turn into some kind of vegetable if I took it up. Doesn't doing nothing for a moment imply calling it quits? What's more, if such a simple method really worked, I told myself, then wouldn't *everyone* be doing it? So, I turned back to the books I was reading and the poems I was writing. But deep down, I was still intrigued.

At the age of twenty-one, I took the plunge. I had started studying philosophy, and my disappointment was as great as the initial enthusiasm that had led me down this path. To be honest, I couldn't cope. I had taken up my studies of the great philosophers in secret, while my parents thought I was studying law. Lying to them left me uneasy, but I also hoped that I might finally succeed in doing something that appealed to me. My grades, however, were mediocre. I found it impossible to read the assigned books, and when I did make the enormous effort to do so, I immediately forgot about the concepts I was supposed to master.

One day, I rang the doorbell of a group of Americans whose address I'd been given; I was feeling completely overwhelmed. An extremely affable man welcomed me and, in just a few words, introduced me to meditation: All I needed to do, he said, was sit down comfortably on my cushion and be present, attentive to what was happening. To put aside my knowledge and skills, and not try to understand, because there was nothing *to* understand. I couldn't believe it: This time I really didn't have anything complicated to do. That was how I meditated for the first time, without yet realizing that I'd been fortunate enough to be initiated by Francisco Varela. The friendly man who'd opened the door was in fact one of the modern world's greatest neurobiologists and a pioneer in exploring the link between science and mindfulness.

On my cushion, I finally experienced true relief. It came as a shock! I was a poor student whose report cards were always full of comments like "could do better," "needs to be severely punished," and "has his head in the clouds." I wanted to do better, but I didn't understand what was required, nor what that had to do with life itself. In elementary school, things weren't so bad. Whenever I had a problem or was sad, I went to see my teacher and then felt better thanks to the caring and trusting relationship we had. But in junior high, we had so many teachers...I had no personal relationships with any of them. I no longer understood anything. We just had to do this or do that. Learn the lesson. Well, I couldn't do it.

But now, for the first time, I didn't have to succeed in accomplishing anything: All I had to do was to be present to what existed, to return to my bodily presence, my breathing, my sensations, my perceptions, what was around me.

At last I felt at home, and I started to attend these group sessions regularly. Sometimes I put a lot of intensity into my practice, even if I was basically being asked to unwind. I experienced sessions during which I was afraid of failing. There was nothing *to* fail, but I didn't really know that yet, and I found it hard to believe. I experienced times when I was worried about being judged, even though no one was there to judge me, and in those moments I felt let down and lost. I could barely breathe because I was focusing so hard on doing well. I didn't yet know that there was nothing to do. I'd have liked someone to tell me "Just stop giving a shit," but that wasn't something people said at the time. I could glean it on occasion, but I still thought I'd misunderstood. Despite myself, I reverted to the mechanisms we put into action whenever we have a task to perform in our everyday lives: I was "paying attention." Attention to not making mistakes, to sitting properly and breathing well. But that was when, suddenly, things would get mixed up, and I'd lose all sense of meditation.

It took me time, and trial and error, before I could finally accept that meditation quite simply means not giving a shit. And that not giving a shit, the golden rule of meditation, should be the leitmotif of any existence. We're conditioned constantly to "do": to cook, work, love, watch a movie, answer the phone. Even when we say, "I'm not doing anything," in reality we're doing many things: We channel surf, we talk to ourselves, we shift from one thought or activity to another, discontinuously, in fear of a moment of silence. Our attention has become fragmented, and we get the impression that if we take a pause we're unproductive, that we're wasting our time rather than accomplishing something vital or fulfilling.

Deep down, meditation is quite simply the art of being: stopping, giving ourselves a break, no longer running but remaining in the present, and anchoring ourselves in our bodies. It is a school of life. Being requires no specific knowledge. Nor does meditation in the way I understand and practice it. In fact, there are no meditation skill sets; the Japanese Zen master Shunryu Suzuki, who lived and taught in the United States in the late 1960s, often repeated that many times beginners are the best at meditation, while experts tend to get lost in overcomplicating it. Meditation, in a sense, means remaining a beginner. Open and curious. You do nothing, and yet plenty of things happen.

I have been trained in a practice that sees meditation as a form of freedom rather than as a technique based on methods or protocol. This is what is now called, quite appropriately, the practice of mindfulness, which implies a total presence rather than a total consciousness. In this respect, meditating is as simple as cleaning your teeth or staring at a fire in a fireplace.

Try it. Sit down. On a cushion, or a chair, it doesn't matter. No posture is imposed or outlawed. Sitting down is not a technique, it's just a very simple way of managing to do nothing, and not being preoccupied by anything. I might also add some commonsense advice: Sit up straight to remain alert, present, and available. Rather than a constraint, I see this as a natural posture: When you watch a movie or attend a conference, it's quite natural to sit up at the most important moments when you don't want to miss anything.

Being upright opens the mind to the fullness of the present. It's no coincidence that we sing more naturally while standing in the shower than when slumped on the couch! Funnily enough, researchers are now exploring this phenomenon. For example, in a recent study, participants were divided into two groups. Researchers asked the first group to slouch with drooping shoulders, as if apologizing. Meanwhile, the second group had to stand up straight, in a posture of success. Then both groups had to carry out the same exercises. In the first group, the participants got stuck and made mistakes. In the second, those standing upright succeeded brilliantly.

Staying upright while meditating can be uncomfortable at first. It takes some time to get used to it, but you must be daring enough to try! You may end up with an aching back or sore legs. Then you should allow yourself to recognize—with care and kindness, and without feeling guilty—that you haven't been sitting "badly," you haven't "failed"; your back or legs just hurt, and this pain doesn't need to be judged. The point is not to torment yourself: If you change your position after a while, you don't deserve to be punished. I'm sometimes asked by meditators if they are "allowed to..." Forget this idea of what's allowed and what isn't, and replace it with freedom. Then who cares if you don't manage to stay upright?

Are you awash with thoughts? So be it. I don't force myself to empty my mind—all that would happen then would be the opposite effect, leading to an uncontrollable flood of images and worries. Instead, I acknowledge what is happening, taking my thoughts as they come. I don't dissect them, nor do I declare war on them or push them out. I consider that all my thoughts, all my perceptions, are a part of meditation. Ultimately, I don't do anything. I just am.

Meditating doesn't mean becoming detached or disembodying yourself. On the contrary, it means opening yourself to the world through your senses, and thus through your body. It means feeling the contact of your feet with the ground, your hands on your thighs, your clothes on your skin. It means hearing a car as it brakes, a passerby who speaks, without trying to understand, or judge, or even put words on what is happening. All it means is being aware: You hear, you see, you're hungry, you're engaged, and soon the sound becomes amplified, it becomes infinite, it becomes poetry...

We can forget that it's not always necessary to explain, under-stand, justify, or criticize ourselves and others. I view meditation as very simple, easy training to embrace this attitude. I don't see this training as an exercise, nor as working on oneself. It's not a rule or a challenge; rather, it's an invitation to let oneself go. It isn't a method for introspection or self-improvement. It isn't about "me, myself, and I." Because "me" isn't just some isolated individual meditating only to stare into my own soul. By meditat-ing, I discover the extent to which I belong to the world. I engage with what *is*, myself included, in an action of kindliness that life has taught us to forget.

Stop meditating...and breathe. Breathing is a natural action that requires no effort. But at the same time, it is an extraordinary phenomenon, the very act of life. Simply by giving myself a break and by breathing, I am alive! Meditating is similar. It is a natural act that allows me to let life return, and through which I become alive once again. It is above all an action that can be adopted at any time, an action that consists of a kind of attention and benev-olence, beyond any judgment. Am I sad, or annoyed? Then I stare my sadness or annoyance in the face...and then I stop giv-ing a shit. Meditation is a form of breathing without guidelines or sanctions. And therein lies its healing power. Breathing means becoming resynchronized with life. Meditating means not giving a shit and allowing ourselves to become human once again.

2

STOP OBEYING

You are intelligent

Resolve no longer to be slaves, and you are free!
—Étienne de La Boétie[1]

When I was a child, my family and I went on vacation in the south of France. At the beach, my parents entered my sister and me into a sand-castle competition. We had an hour, and I set about building a real castle, with keeps and drawbridges. I didn't even finish half of it. My sister, on the other hand, decided to sculpt a ladybug and dot it with strawberry jam (she'd brought a jar from home). She won first prize. I was hugely disappointed: not because she'd won, but because she hadn't followed the instructions. The competition's organizers had rewarded her creativity and, of course, her ability. I do have to admit her ladybug was pretty good.

This anecdote comes back to me every time I'm tempted to blindly follow rules, which inevitably end up just holding me back. Whether these rules have been given to me by others or, even more frequently, are self-imposed (these I call habits), I end up needlessly confining myself to what I think is the right thing, when in fact what I'm doing is actually quite absurd...

Obeying often seems to be the simple and safe solution. When we conform to the rules, we are no longer afraid of getting things wrong; by following instructions to the letter, we're sure of doing well. But without even realizing it, what we're actually doing is consigning ourselves to servitude.

In 1549, the French writer and philosopher Étienne de La Boétie wrote an extraordinary book titled *Discourse on Voluntary Servitude*. This wonderful text was forgotten for centuries, before being brought back in part by Gandhi. In it, La Boétie raises a surprising question: Why do people so readily surrender their freedom and obey others? One of the reasons, he says, is fear of losing the little power we have, no matter how small. The French philosopher Marcel Conche summed it up this way: "Tyrants tyrannize no doubt thanks to a host of little tyrants, who are tyrannized and no doubt tyrannize in turn."[2] Unfortunately, this equation has lost none of its relevance.

Followers that we are, we anticipate orders, and above all, we avoid making any waves. We restrain ourselves, serve our masters (or the mainstream), and even anticipate their desires—and this way we blend in. We obey because we do not want to take risks or get in trouble. We accept censorship, and we even censor ourselves, in pursuit of this goal of conformity. We are persuaded that there is no other way than servitude, abdication, and imitation, for ourselves or for society. We end up forgetting our desire to say no to the absurdity of some of the orders.

Yet we also sense that obeying without any discussion, without understanding why, perhaps even without our consensus, stifles us and stops the intelligence within us from blossoming. We want to say no, but something holds us back. Our education. The way we are raised. The "norms" of society.

As soon as we enter the world, we are encouraged to fit the mold instead of running the risk of adopting our own freedom. At school, we learn to apply ready-made rules, and we are bombarded with the knowledge we will need to find a place in the job market. We are taught neither to think nor to be human, but instead to simply replicate, during tests and exams, the knowledge we have committed to memory. Our education ignores the chaotic world of today and tomorrow, in which we will one day need to move, or change jobs, or develop extremely quickly in our field to keep up with the ever-changing twenty-first century. This is an era in which situational intelligence is in fact desperately needed! To be able to think for ourselves, to question, to read—these are actually skills that are in high demand, both today and in the future. Instead of asking people to conform, we should teach them to think and be free! But society makes this harder than ever.

We confuse learning with conforming, and the push to fit in and improve starts early. Even a playground for a four-year-old turns into "coordination training," while progress in preschool is measured by a "skill-set evaluation" and "mastering the Common Core." An individual's personal fulfillment doesn't matter; it can even be viewed as pure narcissism. All that matters is following the rules. We are like the little boy I was on the beach: We think we're doing well, but instead we're building up the conditions for our failure. We no longer know how to take a step back, to see past the fixed area that surrounds us, the one that we ourselves have set in place. Even though this setting isn't even fixed! The rules are far less rigid than we think.

Of course, it can be risky to leave our environment and take a new path. Yet if we think about it, we *all* experience situations in which we discover resources or knowledge we didn't realize we possessed. Think of a puppy thrown into the water for the first time, who discovers it instinctively knows how to float, and even swim! In seemingly banal situations, even daily ones, we manage to transcend ourselves. We've been brilliant because we've allowed our daring intelligence to express itself.

Great scientists and artists bear witness to such situations— and they reveal a phenomenon that all of us could develop. Albert Einstein revolutionized physics after he transcended conventional rules of science. He was present to what exists, rather than what was preestablished as existing. Thanks to his free spirit, he transformed the way we understand the world. When Isaac Newton was hit on the head by an apple, he chose to leave behind the beaten track that he so easily could have followed, like most of his fellow scientists did. That day, free from constraints, he elaborated the law of universal gravitation. Wassily Kandinsky, on looking at a picture by Claude Monet whose subject he failed to recognize (a haystack), discovered the power of painting and freed himself from the rules and structures he had imposed on himself up until then.

What did Einstein and Kandinsky do that we cannot? They broke the mold, they stopped obeying existing rules—and when they did, something occurred to them that they hadn't necessarily expected.

My grandmother used to make the world's best cheesecake. When I asked her for the recipe, she told me that she used cream cheese, eggs, sugar, flour... then sometimes added grapes, apricots, or other types of fruit. I thought she was being vague on purpose, but she wasn't. Each time, she invented her own way, according to what inspired her, and it was always delicious— sometimes better than usual, sometimes not as good. It's this "not as good" that paralyzes us. We feel reassured by using kitchen scales and following recipes to the letter, without changing a thing. Even if we always repeat ourselves. Even if we never surprise ourselves. Even if we become some kind of robot.

Do you want your exam, interview, or presentation to be successful? Start by giving yourself a break. Free yourself from the molds that are imprisoning you, even though you may not notice them. Discover different strengths, other powers that include the capacity to invent an answer. People interviewing for a job who stick to what they have planned to say, who have rehearsed their speeches, will be thrown off balance when asked an unexpected question. Instead of showing the required presence of mind, they will be stuck in what they have learned, and the rules of how to do well, which they are trying to apply to a T. This obsession with wanting to control everything will stop them from entering into the dance. It will prevent them from giving their best.

I experienced this myself when I gave my first lectures. I so wanted to do well that all I did was stifle myself. I consulted endless books, took notes, and wrote down a text that I read aloud. Everyone was bored, especially me. I was obeying rules I'd made up for myself. One day, I finally realized I should break my own rules. Of course, I still prepare my lectures, but after a time I stop thinking about them. The first time I took the plunge without a written text and only a few notes, it felt like I was throwing myself into the void. The intensity of the experience surprised me. Something that I hadn't foreseen happened. Because I'd started not to give a shit and just trust myself, my lectures at last came to life.

I have often wondered why we persist in submitting to rules that can be absurd, or to finicky protocols that hold us back and stop us from progressing. Perhaps they give us a sense of protection against chaos. In many ways, this is true. I'm sure we cannot live without rules. Nor is it by systematically opposing every rule that we will become creative or alive. How many revolutions have set up rules that are even more rigid than the ones that they were supposedly denouncing? Rioters who take part in protests think that they are free because they attack the rules by using violence, but they remain in a different form of servitude. They are still prisoners of their own molds.

We need a certain number of rules to maintain social cohesion and to structure our daily lives. There are timetables to be followed, tasks to be carried out, a respect for ourselves and for others that needs to be universally accepted. What we should really ask ourselves is: Which ones we should follow, and have we chosen them or not? Are we following them from a fear of being found out, or of taking a risk, or from a real awareness?

I'm emphasizing this point, because my invitation not to give a shit about rules does not mean just fooling around. Quite the opposite. Blindly following certain rules is what causes us to act foolishly.

I'm not suggesting protest for the sake of protest, but rather listening to the intelligence we have within ourselves, and which we quite simply need to rediscover.

I'm not suggesting anarchy, but rather living without a muzzle.

Soccer players who score brilliant goals don't transgress the rules of the game they know so well. Instead, they use the rules to come up with their own way of playing. That is precisely what makes some people so talented. They are good enough to dare, to do the unexpected. They give it their all.

When my sister and I took part in that sand-castle competition, she didn't build a cardboard house, thinking sand was no fun and would get all over her! She adopted the rules of the game, but interpreted them using her own intelligence and creativity. She freed herself from the mold, and she still wasn't eliminated from the competition.

That's right: I'm punctual when I have an appointment, I pay my taxes, I don't ride the Metro without paying the fare, I prepare my lectures. And following these rules frees my mind. I play the social game with its conventions, but I am careful not to become their slave or to be caught up in a routine that would keep me from living fully. I respond to these rules, I conform to them, while trying not to tumble into voluntary servitude.

By not giving a shit, in other words, I allow myself to have an utterly new and vibrant relationship with rules and discipline. I don't conform to a rule because it is a rule; I make it part of me when it makes me freer. If not, I try to question it.

What meditation really teaches us is to find our existing gifts, which will allow us to respond intelligently to a situation. In this respect, the form of meditation I defend is an ethical one: It asks us to face each situation and come up with the right attitude toward it; to abandon the pressure of rules and to refuse the voluntary servitude that leads to tyranny in all its forms.

I have personally suffered from meeting "masters of wisdom" who claim to be able to tell you what you should do. I encountered such masters at a time when I was looking for a path toward freedom. Some of them impressed me, because they were, in fact, profoundly free. But I then had to admit that the groups they had set up did not experience this same freedom. They followed the master's rules and tumbled back into voluntary servitude, backed up by ardent spiritual discourses that made them believe they had been specially chosen.

Around some of these masters, I witnessed their disciples gradually lose control of their lives. Obeying all the time made them lose any confidence in their own resources. They asked for their master's advice for every step they made, and he dictated their "rightful conduct." They had thus ended up annihilating their own intelligence. Not all these masters were bad—some of them were generous and just—but they all shattered any real freedom.

We cannot learn to be, to love, or to decide anything vital while submitting to another person's power.

Deep down, no one can advise anyone else. Each being is different. Each situation is different. Each situation is unique. And the need to think for ourselves concerns all of us.

In London, during the Second World War and the height of Nazism, the French philosopher Simone Weil, who only had a few months more to live, constantly thought about the conditions for new life. It was then that she wrote *On the Abolition of All Political Parties*, in which she compares belonging to a party to belonging to a church, concluding that both are examples of surrendering your intelligence and sense of justice. In both cases, individuals adhere to a thought or belief without knowing all the underlying reasons, and conform to preordained affirmations, which they sometimes know nothing about.

The point is not to stop people from gathering, because groups can provide a valuable foundation for friendship and solidarity to thrive, but instead to protect the freedom of the mind in all places. As she put it:

Nearly everywhere—often even when dealing with purely technical problems—instead of thinking, one merely takes sides: for or against. Such a choice replaces the activity of the mind. This is an intellectual leprosy; it originated in the political world and then spread through the land, contaminating all forms of thinking. This leprosy is killing us; it is doubtful whether it can be cured without first starting with the abolition of all political parties.... When joining the party, [man] therefore also endorses a number of positions which he does not know. In fact, he submits his thinking to the authority of the party.... If a man were to say, as he applied for his party membership card, 'I agree with the party on this and that question; I have not yet studied its other positions and thus I entirely reserve my opinion, pending further information,' he would probably be advised to come back at a later date."[3]

This is what stops our societies from being genuinely democratic.

Meditation, I am told, is intrinsically a technique with its own set of rules. Doesn't it lead us to abandon our freedom? In fact, I would compare its governing rules to punctuality. Being on time doesn't prevent me from being free. On the contrary, it liberates me from the weight of being late, which would clutter my thoughts. Being on time allows me to forget myself so that I'm quite simply present to what is happening. Thanks to their simplicity, the rules of meditation do the same job; their power lies in their simplicity.

What are these rules?

The first rule is to be present to your breathing. This sounds almost stupid! Whatever happens, we breathe without needing to be told how to inhale or exhale. And we breathe all the more easily when we don't think about it, when we don't apply the "right" method for conscious breathing. Being present to the way we breathe naturally, and not through an artificial method, is the first vital step toward a resynchronization with the life inside us. To become one with life once more. There really isn't anything complicated about it.

The second step, which naturally follows, is being open to everything that can be found in a given situation. Here, too, the point is not to force yourself or to obey. Whatever the case, I can hear, I can see, I can feel, and I can think. So all you have to do is breathe, hear, see, and feel. To be present. The problem lies in this simplicity, which is so elementary that it is hard to grasp. It's so elastic that we feel perplexed about the freedom we are given to experience it, in a relaxed, natural way rather than in a mold. It is a tangible experience. In that moment, I am simply open to what is. The rule allows me to limit the field of my attention and thus be more easily present.

While introducing me to this practice, Francisco Varela's first piece of advice was an image I'll never forget: You're in a laboratory, looking into a microscope. Observe everything that happens with curiosity. You don't have to accomplish anything; just watch. The rule is the microscope. The possibility to address your attention. Remain motionless. Be present to your breathing. What matters is everything that this opens you up to, moment by moment.

In this respect, meditation is a radical action: I stop giving a shit, and instead free myself from the rules that arise within me, above all those I impose on myself, generally without anyone expecting anything from me. This is not an exercise, a challenge, or a set of instructions. It is not about success or failure. All that exists are these fifteen minutes, this half hour, sometimes more, during which I set off on an adventure amid all my daily obligations. I stop wanting to meditate, I stop obeying, I do nothing. My entire day takes on a different flavor.

Trusting our own intelligence is a profound experience on which we so often miss out, because we refuse to allot the slightest trust to what we feel. Meditating helps me switch on the antennae I have inside me, just waiting to be deployed; if I can simply accept the fact that I don't know what's going to happen next, if I can open myself up to the unexpected and to the intelligence that will spring up inside me. If I can just not give a shit...

This apprenticeship is never over, because we will continue to make mistakes about freedom. Whatever we do, we shall never be completely free, nor completely in servitude. We are all on the path to freedom, and this path is enthralling. It is the path I have been following for years.

Even if I have now grown up, I still remain the little boy who was asked to build a sand castle and who failed to do so.

3

STOP BEING WISE

Be enthusiastic

*Wisdom is cold, and to that extent stu-
pid.... Wisdom merely conceals life from you.*
—Ludwig Wittgenstein,
Culture and Value[1]

We have a fantastical and rather childish idea of what
wisdom is. We see it as some kind of magical water
we need to sprinkle on our daily lives to dissolve all
our problems and challenges. Then we can get past them easily
and arrive at a contented quietude, 24/7. Wisdom is a kind of
cure-all that we absolutely must acquire, just like the disposable
goods we buy with a single click on the Web.

We look at great sages enviously...we want to become like
them. And quickly, of course. We refuse to listen to the fact

that wisdom is a journey. We don't have enough time to set off on some journey. We want to be Nelson Mandela or the Dalai Lama—now! But this displays a profound misunderstanding; there are no books, lessons, or sessions of meditation or yoga that will provide us with such venerable wisdom. It is the fruit of experience, of efforts and trials, but also of suffering and torments, the fruition of the twenty-seven years Mandela spent in solitary confinement in the South Africa of apartheid, or of the exile of the Dalai Lama and his struggles for the Tibetan people.

We are being deceived if we believe that wisdom is a destination and not a path. In fact, it is a difficult path, and one we certainly do not wish to encumber ourselves with in this era of ease. Then comes discouragement. Despite the "easy" advice that we are given all around, despite our genuine efforts to follow it, we remain irritable, impatient, fragile, and vulnerable. We feel a deep sense of guilt, a sign of our inability to live up to this absurd ideal, while an incredible confusion stops us from understanding what a genuine sage is.

The origin of this confusion is ancient. It dates back to the source of our Western philosophy, to Epicureanism and Stoicism, the two schools of thought developed in Greece in the fourth century BCE. These schools have traditionally been opposed to each other, and yet their objectives were identical: helping people acquire wisdom, and with it serenity, a tranquil soul, and happiness. The paths they offer are in the end quite similar: overcoming the passions, whether fears, desires, anger, or wishes, that disturb our souls so as to be indifferent to pain, problems, and even to death. Such is their ideal—an ideal which, down through the centuries, has lived on and shaped the Western world—that our problems should glide over us without ever touching us. Being a sage would thus mean putting on a kind of impermeable cape to protect us from unhappiness. To exist in supreme indifference to everything.

It is through this deforming prism that we view all other notions of wisdom, including Eastern philosophy, and Buddhism in particular. Buddhism has attracted many Westerners thanks to its promise to "pacify desires" in order to reach Nirvana. This word *nirvana* has entered our everyday vocabulary as a state of perfect beatitude, but in reality, it means "the progressive annihilation of individuals, their return to the inorganic, and death," according to the *General Dictionary of Social Sciences*.[2] All we have retained from the Buddha's path is this watered-down promise, which in truth has nothing to do with the teachings of the Buddha.

Idealizing insensibility is scandalous! It's the opposite of real wisdom. The Buddha, Christ, and Nelson Mandela are excellent counterexamples. These wise heroes weren't all that sleek! They shook up the preordained universe, they got angry, they wept, they said no, they thought concretely about the problems of everyday life and about possible solutions. They excited crowds, slammed doors, made judgments, and tried to create social change, each in his own way. They did not endure without acting, they weren't masochists, and they didn't seek out some Zen-like nirvana state, because they saw how absurd that would be. They exemplified the opposite of a passive view of wisdom, as inherited from the Epicureans and Stoics. They broke the mold of indifference!

We should stop feeling that we're constantly in error, constantly inadequate. The ideal of wisdom nags at us: If we think that wisdom equals a detached, impassive mind, we then see ourselves as pathetic when we are troubled by our little worries and anxiety...but this is completely wrong!

We need to start from who we are. That's true wisdom! Let's start by saying no to these false, destructive commands. We should accept that we do have desires, that we feel fed up, are irritated—and then shake things up when it seems necessary. Let's follow the Romanian philosopher E. M. Cioran, who declared, "We should model ourselves not on the sage but on the child, we should throw ourselves on the ground and cry every time we feel like it. What is more lamentable than to feel like crying and not to dare?"[3]

I have a special place in my heart for the philosopher Ludwig Wittgenstein, because he diverged from our ideal of wisdom and well-being, and he wasn't afraid to forge his own path. Wittgenstein was born in 1889 into a large, wealthy Austrian family, greatly respected in Vienna (Brahms and Mahler came to play piano in his family's townhouse salon, and Klimt painted a portrait of his sister Margaret). After renouncing his family fortune, Wittgenstein moved to England. He taught philosophy in Cambridge and conversed with the greatest minds of the era. One day, he decided to drop everything and go into exile in Norway.

His mentor, Bertrand Russell, reported a conversation he had with him at the time: "I said it would be dark, & he said he hated daylight. I said it would be lonely, & he said he prostituted his mind talking to intelligent people. I said he was mad & he said God preserve him from sanity."[4] In his diaries, Wittgenstein shared how fed up he was with wisdom as it was seen in the West, and with academic hypocrisy, the coldness of intellectual debate, disconnected from the effervescent nature and warmth of reality. He told of his encounters with ordinary people, who genuinely lived with benevolence, love, and concern about using the right words, authentic sages who did not protect themselves artificially in an interior fortress far away from real life, but who instead attempted to become part of it.

Unlike the idea of wisdom as we see it today, in all its terrifying sleekness, I propose a kind of enthusiasm which, through its energy, can cure and change the world. This enthusiasm allows us to leave our comfort zone, to stand outside ourselves, and move toward something greater. "All the greatest things we know have come to us from neurotics," wrote Marcel Proust. "It is they and they only who have founded religions and created great works of art. Never will the world be conscious of how much it owes to them, nor above all of what they have suffered in order to bestow their gifts on it. We enjoy fine music, beautiful pictures, a thousand exquisite things, but we do not know what they cost those who wrought them in sleeplessness, tears, spasmodic laughter, rashes, asthma, epilepsy."[5] We have forgotten this, by pitting the challenges we all experience against the "purity" of a pseudospirituality that is lukewarm, ethereal, and inherently morbid.

I recognize that enthusiasm also includes disorder and up-heaval. And how marvelous! It was the Buddha who cared nothing for conventions, and who fled from the comfort of his palace to join a group of ascetics, and then left this group after giving them a piece of his mind, and shook up the order of society by refusing the system of castes and privileges of the Brahmans. What a scandal! It was Jesus who overturned the tables of the merchants in the Temple, which was a crazy thing to do in what was then Judaism's most sacred place. What a sacrilege! It was Mandela who took up arms, encouraging a revolution against the absurdity of South African apartheid. What infamy! Think of the sages and great masters who address crowds, as Socrates did, and who provoke respectable people, like Diogenes, who slept in a barrel; when Alexander the Great came to see him and asked what he wanted, he replied, "Stand out of my sunlight."

There's a form of provocation in true wisdom, because it confronts what we don't want to see when dealing with this subject: work, money, violence, sexuality, and challenges. In other words, life. But what other topics would be worth attracting the wisdom and philosophies of every continent and era? Pseudo-sages retreat into their inner fortresses, which are sleek and comfortable, where nothing seems to affect them. They pass on to their disciples one of Charles Baudelaire's injunctions: "Be wise, Oh my sorrow, be calmer."[6] But true heroes do not make wisdom synonymous with quietude. They do not seek to transcend the world, but to espouse it. What would the Buddha, Jesus, or Socrates say to the naïve, disembodied sages of today, who are busier praying, meditating, and providing sugarcoated advice, than liberating us from violence, in all its forms, and denouncing the dictatorship of profitability?

I am tired of being asked, because I'm involved in meditation: "How can I become Zen?" As if this question had any meaning! Why am I not asked: "How can I become a little more alive?" That is the real challenge. Our challenge. Enthusiasts are called into the world. They know they will receive blows, become irritated, fight back, get angry, sometimes rightly so, sometimes unjustly, but that doesn't matter—they are ready to roll up their sleeves and get going. There is more truth in their emotions than in all those masters with aloof gazes, which they no doubt think contribute to their caricatures of dignity.

I am horrified by the vision of wisdom that is presented to us, including in mainstream media, of what boils down to a scientifically validated means for taking refuge in a small comfort zone. This kind of wisdom is just another form of consumerism. Instead of buying some item or other in a supermarket, I'll get some wisdom. As if it were outside of us. I'll buy something, so as to feel better, but once I've bought this product, I'll no longer feel satisfied. I will immediately need something else. Whatever is offered next. Such deception makes us ever more dependent, and gives us the illusion that we aren't up to the situation, that we're failures! Isn't this, in fact, the very rationale of consumerism?

So, learn not to give a shit, and you'll find that wisdom is already there, inside you. Please stop tormenting yourself with this impossible quest: Wisdom is not some unattainable Grail; it dwells only in the here and now, inside us all. Being wise doesn't imply denying who I am, so as to reach a perfection that doesn't exist, but rather opening myself up to who I am, imperfect as I am, as we *all* are.

Stop meditating if you're doing it to learn to "let go," as per the current trend, because you won't be able to. Meditating doesn't mean calming down, it means engaging with your own life.

Meditating doesn't mean distancing yourself from the earthly world, or turning your gaze away from your everyday life. On the contrary, it involves embracing everything that constitutes existence, including sex, money, work, shitty situations, and joy.

Real wisdom consists neither in burying our emotions nor in exhibiting them. It entails engaging with them, listening to them, and recognizing what they are saying, so you can ultimately distinguish truth from falsehoods. At times I get angry, for instance, when I see new publications, or TV and radio shows, that present meditation as a method to help us become more efficient, calm, and successful. When they add that this fact has been proven, and that it increases the productivity of workers who practice it, my blood boils. What a disgrace!

I know no better way to free yourself from a symptom than to embrace it fully. Going to the bitter end of a phobia or an anxiety, facing up to it, even if this scares us—*especially* if it scares us. Am I angry? I forget the command to let go, which is itself the opposite of letting go. I don't let go. I don't give a shit! I do nothing, I *let* what is happening happen, without repressing it. I don't judge my anger, I don't comment on it, I don't authorize it, but I don't forbid it, either: I take the risk of experiencing it.

I taste it, even if it hurts me. What often follows is relief, not the calm we try to enforce by artificially stifling what we are living through.

This is the very basis of meditation: It's neither herbal tea nor a magic pill, but instead real work on our sorrows, confusion, and emotions. It teaches us to observe them as they are, like a doctor examining his or her own wounds. It means facing up to everything that is stopping us from truly not giving a shit, greeting what is hurting us, and welcoming the life inside us. I will learn far more about myself than if blindly obeying the command to avoid it all, which stems from Stoic and Epicurean wisdom.

A form of peace lies at the end of this journey. But only if we don't turn the journey into a new way of brutalizing ourselves! That is the crux of the story. In the name of wisdom, we torture ourselves and become ever more inauthentic. As we obviously fail to become bland, calm, detached, and impassible, we pretend to be so. In reality, we accept a path of confusion and disorientation.

A parable in the Gospels tells the story of an impure spirit (call it anger, or anxiety) that leaves a man behind to seek rest in a dry place. He fails to find one and comes back to the man's house, which is now empty and swept clean (by what might be considered the commands of wisdom). "Then goeth he, and taketh with himself seven other spirits more wicked than himself, and they enter in and dwell there: and the last state of that man is worse than the first" (Matthew 12:43–45 KJV).

What a magnificent parable! If, when I want to be calm, I

chase away my anger, or my anxiety, without first having recognized or made peace with them, they will become even worse, no matter what precautions I take to avoid them. Wisdom, as it is currently understood, is then nothing more than a bandage, which may provide superficial protection but certainly does not act against the infection. Quite the opposite! If we try to control everything, we may keep going for a while, but ultimately we'll fall apart.

Furthermore, despite popular belief, not all anger is blind. Some forms of anger can be just, and meditation tries to identify and let them express themselves. Gandhi emphasized the fact that we shouldn't be ashamed of our anger. He claimed it was a profound energy that could help us transcend ourselves. What we should be ashamed of, however, is our way of misusing it when we don't understand it.

Deep down, it is also anger that gives us the strength to teach, to write, to be at the service of something greater than ourselves. Our anger is surely no more than a drop in the ocean, but we know the story of the hummingbird who carried a tiny drop of water in its beak to put out a forest fire: "I'm doing what I can," it answered to those who made fun.[7] Daring to denounce is often wiser than prudently withdrawing into your shell.

The omnipresent order to become wise blinds us to the suffering of the world, the isolation lurking around the corner, everything that is wrong with our planet. It makes us forget the present and aspire to a distant tranquility. It stops us from connecting with the here and now. It harnesses the cart before the horse. What genuine tranquility can I aspire to if I have forgotten to live, and have instead shut myself in an ivory tower?

So, learn to give yourself a break, and liberate the enthusiasm within you, without ever being ashamed of it. It's proof that you're alive!

4

STOP BEING CALM

Be at peace

Which is more difficult: holding back a horse, or letting it run and, because the horse we are holding back is ourselves—which is more unpleasant: being held back or allowing our strength to run free? To breathe, or not to breathe?

—Marina Tsvetaeva,
Letter to the Amazon[1]

Being calm in all circumstances: what an idea! Staying calm implies controlling yourself and never expressing too vigorously your anger or sorrow, your joy or desires.

It sounds like an appealing promise at first, but this command in fact forbids us from being who we are and transforms us into uniform sheep. Being calm is like a drug. Whatever happens, even if it's hurtful, "Calm down" is our new mantra. We forget that only death can freeze us into absolute calmness. The calm we extol is the very opposite of life.

One day, while teaching meditation, I was emphasizing over and again the absurdity of this command when one of the participants retorted: "But I need to be calm to be able to get in touch with myself and make a decision." She continued, "I meditate to be calm, and I don't see what the problem is." I suggested we go back over the true meaning of the words we use. *Calm*, the dictionary tells us, comes from the Occitan *calma*. This naval term describes an absence of wind, which sometimes consigned sailors to inactivity, that is, unemployment. When the sea is calm, it's impossible to move! Calm is the absence of movement, a static immobility.

Of course, I love and appreciate those moments when I feel in harmony with the world, and time seems to stand still at last. I delight in that feeling of plenitude and relief, obviously, and the longer it lasts, the *more* I delight in it. But I also know that saying "Calm down" never calms anyone down. The feeling I want to talk about is not a command; it comes to us as a bonus, or a gift. It is acquired.

I call this feeling peace. *Peace*, the dictionary tells us, derives from the old Indo-European root *pehg*, which can be found in the Latin *pax* and above all in the verb *pango*, and the Greek *pegnumi*, which means "to repair, adjust, and work." *Peace* implies an effort to bring things together as they should be. In other words, it is the exact opposite of calming down. In this sense, meditation pacifies, but it does not calm. And that's a good thing!

A feeling of peace has nothing to do with this sleek, perfect ideal that has been conveyed in the West since the days of Epicurus and the Stoics. It is not a calmness based on a narrow, numb, dull (and inherently false) vision of life. Peace does not imply protecting yourself from the tumult of emotions, life, waves, and stormy weather. On the contrary, it includes them in its fullness. It is not upset by minor annoyances—missing a train or an appointment, getting sick at the wrong time, not receiving a letter we've been eagerly awaiting. It is not an absence of trouble but the capacity to patiently and gently engage with the bulk of reality, including with our own rage, or sorrow, whose existence we also must recognize rather than deny. I don't stifle my sorrow, or avoid it, because this could be incredibly violent. Nor do I judge it. I am quite simply present to it. I don't order myself to calm down. I don't give a shit! I add nothing to the experience I'm going through.

I know that some might find the idea of rejecting calm to be jarring, especially when expressing emotions in any lively way has become taboo. At a time when society tells us to be cogs in the machine—perfectly calm, perfectly smooth, truly effective, smiling, with neither emotions nor problems, ever-successful, from morning till night, I'm aware that those who accept and flaunt their differences often end up being thrown out of the machine entirely. So let's play this game a little— while remaining aware that it is just a game, albeit often an extremely violent one. Let's accept that we should not always be nice, or please everyone, or be loved all the time, by everybody.

From junior high to high school, between the ages of thirteen and seventeen, I don't recall ever having spoken to my classmates. I didn't understand their games. Once, the gym teacher insisted that I play soccer with the others (my worst nightmare!). He placed me at the far end of the field, which initially reassured me, given that everyone else was playing on the opposite side. But then, suddenly, they all ran toward me and passed me the ball. I was terrified. Paralyzed. The ball hit me in the face. I lost my glasses. I wanted to cry. I looked like an idiot.

I suffered a lot from such moments, such situations when I seemed "weird"—as I was called. But when I finally accepted the fact that I was weird, I started making warmer connections with other people.

Even today, I don't feel completely at ease in many social situations. For example, when I go to a wedding—something I avoid as much as possible—I don't like sitting at a table with people I don't have much to say to. I don't like the moment when we all have to raise our hands, sing in unison, and embrace. Such situations bother me, but I've ended up accepting them—thanks to the fact that I can accept that I'm a serious person. Yes, I'm serious. And too bad if people don't like that.

Let's stop feeling guilty if we don't always manage to present a sleek and socially suitable façade—the façade of a robotized ideal. Bear in mind that a perfect harmony, the rippleless sea we aspire to, is meaningless, and that it leads to the disappearance of all life. "It is dangerous to preach humility to feeble souls. This distances them even more from themselves. Someone who is rigid, and turned inwards, can become aware of his destiny only by rebelling," said the poet and writer René Daumal.[2] He was a leading figure of the Great Game ("le Grand Jeu"), an early twentieth-century movement in France that aimed at a genuine spiritual and metaphysical revolution.

We no longer dare to say no, nor express a contrary opinion, for fear of being wrong or making waves. We bury our desire to say no instead of making it explicit and moving on. When discussions become heated, we cut them short with a shifty "Calm down," which actually means "Shut up." In the name of this ideal of calm, we allow absurdity to take the upper hand, wounds to fester, a malaise to build up, and lies to dominate. By censoring and stifling ourselves, we turn into pressure cookers that implode in a silent burnout. We run away from crises, even though they often call us into question in a healthy way.

Let's play the game, but without taking refuge in our bubbles; we have no right to do so, in a century full of so much suffering and horror. I am often asked, as a long-term practitioner of meditation, if I am happy—in other words, if I've reached the state of calm that we associate with happiness. My answer is always the same: That is not the question. I didn't decide to meditate so as to take shelter from the world, but instead to better fit inside it. I didn't start meditating to eliminate my own suffering, with the issues and anxiety it involves, but to better enter into the dance of reality. I don't seek the comfort of a selfish, spiritual calm, where I'd be on the side of goodness, and then look at others with compassion. This temptation, which exists in all religious, spiritual, and philosophical traditions, seems to lead us astray. A real form of wisdom does exist, but it is quite different from the adulterated version that's being pushed in front of us, and it can provide a deep happiness, one that is utterly different from our conventional ideas.

Meditation is universally presented as the finest way to calm down. So I'll state it again clearly: I don't try to calm down by meditating. When sitting on my cushion, I don't even try to relax. While practicing, such ideas are alien to me. I am happy simply to place myself on the earth, to feel in contact with the ground, and to be present to everything that is happening, including any storm that might surge up inside me. I make no judgments about the thoughts that I should be having. I don't terrorize myself with commands of any sort. I don't imagine that I'm entering a refuge, where serenity awaits. I don't even look for it. I don't look for anything. I'm just there, sitting, attentive: to a bee buzzing, a car horn, my body, my being, or my tension, if I feel tense.

At the beginning, such a reversal of normal patterns can seem radical, and we can have the feeling that we no longer have any markers. We are unused to having absolutely nothing to do, so as to make something occur. But then what does occur is enormous: It is life.

How wonderful it is to quite simply become a living being again!

The goal of meditation is to lead us to engage with reality, while giving ourselves a break so that we can willingly experience whatever it is we're going through. Calmly or not, it doesn't matter. By simply being present, I synchronize myself with what is. When riding a horse, I don't go tense when it starts to gallop: I follow its movements and try to accompany them. I don't observe my thoughts as they pass, waiting for the final one to vanish. I don't try to create a vacuum within myself, or around me. I'm here. That's all. The experience of peace then comes as a bonus—precisely because I *don't* reject the wind when it blows. Wanting to be calm means never being at peace.

Because it allows waves, meditation doesn't crush or suffocate me. Because it permits disorder, it is serene. I am open to everything that is happening, quite freely. I can be sad, I can be unhappy or moved, I can shed tears, but I am profoundly appeased. I don't need to be calm to reach this state. All I need is truly not to give a shit. If I care too much, then I am necessarily more tolerant of all sorts of attacks, which I no longer see as attacks but as waves; and beyond the waves, what I see is the ocean.

I'm often asked which is the best way to practice—in other words, which process of meditation will be most efficient. I always answer with a personal anecdote. At school, I was a poor student in every subject, except eighth-grade history and geography. The reason is very simple: I had a teacher, René Khawam, who was incredibly kind. He had a strong impact on me and I understood him. His teaching method wasn't better than anyone else's, but I found him inspiring, because he was so enthusiastic and genuine. As a result, I was passionate about his class.

Well, the same thing applies to meditation. The best way to

practice is to use the method that means something to you. The one which, thanks to the right transmission, connects you not only with your humanity but also with the entirety of humanity. Which makes you want to do it again, to continue, to go further down this path.

I respect different approaches to meditation. But from experience, I now understand that its simplest forms best suit our Western psyches, which are different from psyches forged in the East. Rituals, incense, and statuettes put most of us off, because they make us feel the weight of dogmas and religions. This complicates something that should remain simple.

We also need to understand what we're doing, what meditation is, and what it asks us to do—here lies the true rationality of the practice. It is impossible to feel content with the blind repetition of an exercise.

In the interest of simplicity, rigor, and openness, I eventually eliminated from my practice and teaching the three most widespread approaches to meditation.

The first approach consists of observing our thoughts as they cross our minds, like clouds passing over the summit of a mountain. The idea is not to hang on to any of them, not to linger, but to let them pass by, down to the very last one. There then comes a moment, supposedly, when there are no clouds left to block the sky. The idea behind this method isn't bad, but those who practice it end up extremely bored, and with good reason. It is far too awkward and imprecise. It encourages us to distance ourselves too much from what we are experiencing and it's much too intellectual. The point of meditation is not to observe, but to pay attention to our entire being, with all our heart. This is something completely different.

The second technique offers a certain number of exercises so as to try to control our minds. Meditators intentionally empty out their thoughts and create a void around themselves. Some people choose to focus on a statue of the Buddha, or the flame of a candle as their focal point, excluding anything else. Others concentrate on their breathing in an intense, even aggressive, way. The aim here is clearly to find this idea of calm, perceived as the total absence of thought, and based on the avoidance of all problems.

This often leads to a state of paranoia. I've known several anxious meditators who would repeatedly experience the incursion of their thoughts during the session, much to their frustration. Often these dedicated meditators would seek the optimal situations for their practice, some of them even committing to several weeks of strict meditation retreats. And for a while, away from the bustle of everyday life, it worked. But many soon found they'd lost their enthusiasm and vigor for meditation. They'd experienced, in this cocoon, such an extreme peace that the return to normality and its inevitable compromises seemed unbearable. The world appeared even more aggressive than before! A quest for calm had robbed them of any true peace. They lived in fear of losing what they had managed to briefly encounter.

Finally, there is a third, more religious approach, where meditation consists of melting into the divine. Personally, I meditate so as to anchor myself more firmly in the present moment. Not to fly off into the heavens.

The approach I favor, and which I've been teaching for years, is simple. It involves not wanting anything, not seeking anything, and developing an attitude of *total presence* to what is, including our thoughts, just as they are in the fullness of the present. In other words, talking to the child within and asking it to abandon any final goal. For years, no matter how I proceeded, I saw many meditators become tense from feeling they weren't going to succeed. Repeating that it wasn't a question of success didn't work. No one listened. One day, I told them, "You just need to stop giving a shit!" And then at last, they started to meditate and to discover the true meaning of peace.

Let me explain this point with an image: Thoughts, sounds, and sensations are like waves on the ocean's surface, both high and low; no matter how high they are, they don't stop us from seeing the ocean or experiencing its depth. Similarly, being at peace means not running away from confusion or disorder. I may be sad, I may cry or roll up in a ball of sorrow, but it doesn't matter that much; it will pass. I am not defined by my sorrow nor does it own me; I am far more than it is. So I can experience sorrow without controlling or rejecting it. It even has its place in my meditation. By looking at the ocean, I end up no longer distinguishing the waves. I have not tried to calm down, but instead I have aimed to be at peace. And now I feel lighter...

What is peace? At the beginning of the twentieth century, Silouan, a poor Russian peasant, went to Greece on a quest to find God during a retreat in a monastery on Mount Athos. He was an ardent ascetic, and visitors came from afar to meet him.

He had been made starets, or patriarch, of the monastery. Father Silouan was widely cited as a model, but deep down, he was truly desperate. One day, while deep in prayer, he heard Christ say to him: "Leave your mind in hell, but do not despair."[3] This idea is precisely the opposite of what we seek out today, frantically consuming meditation sessions, yoga lessons, and books about well-being or personal development. It demolishes our model of being calm as a comfortable, protective dimension—a dimension that includes a complete misunderstanding of what great spiritual beings experience. Even in his refuge on Mount Athos, this great ascetic was not sheltered from his emotions. But it is at the very center of suffering, and even of hell, that serenity can blossom.

True peace is something we can discover at the very heart of our anxiety; it isn't isolated from emotions, passion, or insecurity. Peace does not arise from a total control over who we are, but instead from the transformation of one's reality. For instance, take a sick child who has a fever and is in pain. When he moans, his mother holds his hand. She loves him. The child's suffering doesn't go away, but it is transformed. He's still in pain, but he feels love and support. His space opens out into something other than sickness, something even stronger. The illness is still there, of course, but it has now become something else. He now feels safe.

Meditation as I understand, practice, and transmit it, is a way to reach this transmutation. It does not wipe out emotions but transforms them, opening us up to benevolence, or a form of peace. It takes us toward a different relationship with the small and larger problems of everyday life. Peace of this kind does not wipe out our issues or bypass them. It is another way of perceiving them and, above all, of engaging with them, whenever they occur. Meditation as I understand it is a path toward exaltation, passion, and action.

5

STOP HOLDING
YOURSELF BACK

Desire!

*Heaven belongs to the impetuous who won't
wait.*

—Lou Andreas-Salomé[1]

How did we come to believe that wisdom, philosophy,
and spirituality (especially Buddhism) are well-beaten
paths that turn us into beings without any desire, and
thus without torment? By what disastrous process have we cut
our universe into two halves, one of which seethes with Eros and
love, while the other is a placid wisdom—one that is increasingly
removed from our genuine concerns? Once again, we have inherited this, no doubt, from the Stoics and Epicureans of ancient
Greece, who built up a false dichotomy between calm and action, passivity and resolve.

It's strange, because philosophy is not ascetic, but erotic. In the invaluable *Symposium*, Plato declares that the greatest example of Eros is not a pretty young boy or girl, but Socrates, an ugly old man: "he who does the most for mankind, and inspires daring."[2] Such an Eros is "far from being delicate and beautiful, as most people think; on the contrary it is crude and harsh, it walks barefooted, it is homeless, it always sleeps on the floor, on a hard surface, it sleeps outside at night, beside doors and pathways...it is always in a state of need."[3] It sets us aflame with desire that draws us away from the cave described by Plato in his *Republic*, in which we are chained up facing a wall of shadows, which we mistake for reality. These shadows are not real. Eros has the power to break our chains and take us out of our comfort zones so that we can breathe freely and thus throw ourselves into the chaos of the world.

The Buddhism that I've studied and experienced is by no means an enemy of desire. It comes from the Buddha, who lived to the age of eighty, whose immense passion was to alter the world order, to help all living beings, and who managed to do so thanks to his relentless activism. It is true that the Buddha built his teaching on the discovery that we need to eliminate the *trishna* in us. A mistranslation, still widely believed today, has led us to think *trishna* means "desire." But, literally, it means "an overwhelming thirst." It is the "ever more" that we now see in consumerism: an unquenchable thirst that is the opposite of desire.

Extinguishing the *trishna* within us does not mean living as if we were dead. Quite the opposite: It means rediscovering the brimming source of life, and a deep sense of desire. Quite clearly, Buddhism does not ask its faithful followers to cut themselves off from life. I know only one system that does so: the religion of management, which sees each person's desire as a brake on their efficiency. It imposes on us a rhythm and the terrible diktats of profitability. A good employee should want what the market states. We should consume according to the market's commands, and produce accordingly as well.

The desire I'm talking about here is not consumerist thirst. It has nothing to do with wanting a new car, or a trip to the Caribbean. This desire, my genuine desire, will remain forever, at least in part, unknown to me. It is the force of life that carries me forward, which often surprises me but always liberates me. It is a feeling that grips me profoundly, and though I can't control it, I always see it as being deeply my own when I recognize it. This desire removes me from myself and allows me to discover the meaning of my real self. It supposes that something about my deepest existence has now become radiant.

I know this may sound surprising, but our true desires are not concealed in the inner coils of our egos. I cannot identify them by retreating inward so as to question and understand myself: On the contrary, I can encounter them only by committing myself to the world. Desire means being summoned by something that awakens us.

Researchers into positive psychology have carried out a study of what real desire (the kind that truly moves us) might be. They asked men and women of different ages to note down every day the instant when they felt happiest, and give it a score from one to ten, according to their feelings. At the beginning, the answers were dull: "at home, watching TV," "while having a bath," "when out shopping." Then things grew more focused and surprising: The highest scores were given to activities involving the will to live up to an inescapable desire. For some of them, it might be a piano lesson, with a particularly difficult piece to play. For others, something that was relatively hard to organize but had been, despite the obstacles. For others still, an involved group commitment. These moments of happiness all had something in common: a desire for accomplishment. This desire takes us out of our comfort zones to lead us further toward other people and other places, toward what is right and what is greater than our me-myself-and-I attitude. That is the real meaning of desire. Desire comes when I am no longer looking at myself, but instead at what needs to be done. In other words, strangely enough, when I follow such a desire, I couldn't care less about the rest. I'm so passionate about what I'm doing that I forget myself!

The psychologist Mihály Csikszentmihályi calls these experiences "optimal," because they fit as closely as possible with a state of "complete absorption" he has defined as "flow." What triggers them? "The positive aspects of human experience—joy, creativity, the process of total involvement with life," as he put it.[4] When the people who go through these kinds of experiences are asked what they felt, most answer: "Nothing." Once freed from the false obligations that alienate them from their true selves, they merge with the object they are focusing on.

Let's pay attention to what is calling out to us! Let's take a moment to take some distance from the commands, social pressures, or projects that our parents or entourage have for us. It isn't easy for us to stop following them, for we aren't fully aware of what we are doing. I needed a lot of training before I could give myself a break, to admit that I had every right to be strange, to engage with the idea that I am strange, and to realize that, deep down, I'm not strange. I'm quite simply unique, with my own desires, just as all of us are unique. All we need to do is recognize it and then move on.

No need to make a big deal about it.

I can't repeat this enough: Listening to who we are, and to what appeals to us, does not mean being introspective. Listening to ourselves is, just like meditation, terribly simple. It's an approach that does not involve turning toward the abyss of our inner selves, but rather observing, with a receptive neutrality, what is happening to us, affecting us, speaking to us. It means becoming curious once more, and learning to see outside ourselves while taking in the earth and sky around us.

Discovering the meaning of desire in this way frees us from the moralizing, guilt-inducing command to be less selfish and more altruistic. No, just take the time to listen to what is calling to you, and spontaneously, you will emerge from yourself, be attentive to others, and become engaged. Ask yourself, quite simply, what you want. Someone who becomes involved in an association to help combat violence against women or to aid the illiterate doesn't do so from some altruistic sense of duty, but because it appeals to them, speaks to them, makes them feel more alive and happier.

Stay free. That is the great lesson of desire: It tells us gently and softly to open up even more so that our world becomes increasingly livable. Stop holding yourself back, and desire away.

6

STOP BEING PASSIVE

Learn to wait

Summer might come after. It does come. But it comes only to the patient ones, who are there as if eternity lay in front of them.

—Rainer Maria Rilke,
Letters to a Young Poet[1]

We have a very strange view of taking action. We consider it something that produces an immediately measurable result: tidying up a cupboard, filling in an Excel spreadsheet, moving to a new house, opening a bottle of wine, killing enemies with a video game console. Otherwise, we feel that nothing is happening.

Taking action is, in a sense, busying oneself. In this respect, being overbooked is the greatest proof of success. Why? What's the point? We no longer wonder about such things, because we obviously don't have the time. When I think about this drive to keep busy, the businessman character from Antoine de Saint-Exupéry's *The Little Prince* comes to mind. When the Little Prince gets to the fourth planet, the businessman is absorbed in adding columns of numbers. "I have so much work to do!" he says to the Little Prince.[2] When the Little Prince tries to start a conversation, he states, "I'm a serious man. I can't be bothered with trifles!" The businessman is adding up the number of stars in the sky so that he can own them and get rich. And, once he does own them, he counts them over and over again, then locks his accounts up in a drawer. He has never admired a star, smelled a flower, or loved anyone. He has never taken his eyes off his accounts. He repeats that he is a "serious person." "That's amusing," replies the Little Prince. "But not very serious... grown-ups are certainly quite extraordinary."[3]

According to our understanding of action, the businessman is extremely active, and the Little Prince is just an idler. Executives who run from one pointless meeting to some other hectic appointment pride themselves on being extremely active. Artists, too, as long as their canvases are profitable on the art market. Otherwise, they will have made nothing of their lives. We are like the patient who continually claps his hands until the psychiatrist asks: "Why are you clapping?" The patient then answers: "To chase away the elephants!" "But there aren't any elephants here," the psychiatrist answers. And the patient replies, while continuing to clap: "See, it's working!"

We laugh at this story without realizing that we are all that patient clapping, that we constantly take up absurd, mechanical activities that are meaningless except that they give us the impression we're being active, when in fact we're being terribly passive. If our children get bad grades, we feel we're taking action when we say: "Do your homework." If our partner never clears the table, we feel that by constantly requesting they help ("Don't just stand there"), we're being active, in the hopes the message will finally reach them. There are countless examples. Take teachers who press on with their syllabi, without reaching out to their students or making sure that they've understood the material. Such teachers may have worked intensely, but have they actually achieved anything? If their students complain that the class is boring, it is with good reason. And what about employees who are up to their eyes in projects without having an overview of them, or with no sense of the people who lie behind all the numbers involved?

Running around like a hamster doesn't mean being active!

Our concept of action is shortsighted. And it's difficult for us to see beyond this, because we're prisoners of a ridiculous dichotomy between activity and passivity.

We need to reexamine our conception of time. Can we really measure time with a stopwatch? Is time really at play when I count the number of files I've dealt with in one morning or how many charts I've filled out in an hour? Real time is not measured by clocks. It cannot be measured. It is not seen in formatted "processes." Time is not normative. We all have our own time, which is sometimes so full we forget about it.

One day, a little boy asked me: "Why does time go by more

quickly when I'm playing than when I'm doing homework?" What a deep and intelligent question! Real time is what we need to learn to walk, read, and progress. It is what we need so as to allow ourselves to exist. This is not the time of "means" as produced by data banks, which, in fact, correspond to nothing at all. Means are just means and never ends in themselves.

These obsessions stop us from engaging with real time, that is, our own time. The result is that we live in constant impatience, in fear of social dictates, fixated on writing an article in an hour, learning a new language in three months, or turning over a new leaf after a separation of five or six weeks.

At the same time, I often hear it said that meditation is a passive pause during an active life, a break from agitation, an instant of emptiness that is inserted between two frantic tasks. It's true that while I meditate I'm sitting, I don't speak, and I don't move—at first glance, nothing is happening. I'm quite simply attentive, like a doctor who motionlessly listens to a patient for some time before deciding on the necessary treatment. But no one would accuse the doctor of being passive! Rather, doctors are lauded for the attentiveness that allows them to make a full diagnosis; they are thanked for having devoted their time, as opposed to other doctors who might be under so much time pressure that they end up recommending a treatment while only half-listening to their patients, their next appointment always in mind. The way a doctor listens is considered an action because we deem it as having a "purpose" (making a diagnosis, prescribing treatment, etc.).

When I meditate, I act exactly like a conscientious, humane

doctor. I carry out a profound, genuine action: I stop where I am, I remain silent, and I give myself a break in order to be more open to reality. I accept the idea of waiting and listening to life in its effervescence. I'm not uptight about something happening or obsessed with something I expect. I'm waiting for neither a bus nor an e-mail. I'm waiting without waiting for anything. I offer myself up to this wait for what might happen without knowing in advance what it will be. The wait does not mean indifferently forgetting everyday life, or ignoring its problems and difficulties. It is just a wait during which I "do" something for a change.

Looking back, I realize meditating has taught me to take risks. I've built myself up. I've acquired courage and determination. I've become a little more who I really am. For all these reasons, I think that meditating—like coming to a stop, looking at a work of art, or walking in the mountains—is a way of finally being active. A way of doing something decisive that transforms us, even in a world that, despite being frenetically agitated, is far more passive, and that pushes us far too much toward passivity.

Stop being passive, and reestablish a relationship with your being and your life. Become committed. Taking genuine action means allowing something to be, allowing a meaning to blossom. I view activity like the psychoanalyst Henry Bauchau, who in his book *L'Enfant bleu* (*The Blue Child*) retraced fifteen years he'd spent working with Orion, a young psychotic patient. For fifteen years, the therapist waited for Orion to emerge from his shell and reveal the treasures that the therapist sensed lay inside him. Fifteen years of therapy sessions, during which nothing presumably happened, in the usual sense of the term. Fifteen years during which Orion gradually opened up, in an objectively invisible way, to speech, creation, and art, which was to become his profession, until at last he found his place in the real world.

This ability to wait, which is not passive but deeply active, is based on trust: I don't know how things are going to turn out, but I remain attentive, open, and present to what is happening. I give myself the right not to know, not to be impatient, but to be ready for what will occur. I trust life. I deliver myself to it, for it will help me if I let it work within me.

A friend who had lost her husband said to me: "I can't get over him and move on"—this was her reaction to the terrible decree that there is a time to grieve and a time to move on. The more she clung to this obligation, and the more she tried desperately to make that step, the less she succeeded in doing so. She wanted some advice to move the process along, an exercise she could do, a book she could read, an action she could carry out to feel that she was doing something. I no doubt surprised her by telling her that she should simply give herself permission to live out her grief. Why struggle against reality? We're bound to lose.

Being active does not mean being busy. It does not mean running around in all directions vainly to give others (and ourselves) the impression that we're doing something. It means building deep down, on rock and not on sand. It means understanding, finding a new answer to a situation that seems insoluble. I'm often passive when I'm busying myself. I become truly active when I dare to stop everything, to wait and trust. A doctor needs to take the risk of remaining still for a moment without knowing what is happening. We do, too. It is under this condition that perhaps something completely different, something I'd never thought of before, may appear to me as being obvious and lead me out of the dead end where I've driven myself.

7

STOP BEING CONSCIOUS

Be present

What hells must man still endure before he re-alizes that he is not his own creation?
—Martin Heidegger[1]

During the seventeenth century, in the midst of European intellectual fervor, the French mathematician and philosopher René Descartes set off on a quest for a form of knowledge that was as sure as faith—which at the time seemed to be the highest possible form of certitude. He was full of wonder at mathematics, which he saw as an "admirable science," because of the evident clarity of its reasoning, which addressed our conscious minds without any intrusion from the imprecise prism of perception or sensations.[2] He saw this consciousness as immaterial, working independently from the body, which was just a functional machine. This is the well-known principle of dualism, which has deeply marked Western thought and our relationship with existence.

I may doubt the existence of my body, said Descartes, but not of my mind, the essence of my being. I am a consciousness, and this consciousness makes up my individuality. It is an entity apart, a citadel that is alien to the outside world, free from any relationship with matter, including the body and the senses, which, he claimed, often delude us. It is the basis of all certitudes, "the native land of truth,"[3] on which our knowledge of all things relies. It is thus the precondition for knowing, and it tends to control everything, because it is the path that gives access to the truth: thanks to it alone, human beings can become "masters and possessors of nature."[4]

Descartes took apart the way humanity had functioned since its beginnings, that is to say, living in symbiosis with the cosmos, the world, reality, other people, our own bodies and what they tell us. According to him, consciousness does not need all this clutter in order to exist. I am surer of my consciousness (the well-known "I think, therefore I am") than of the exterior world, he claimed. And we believed him!

We have succumbed to the idea that consciousness is a little island cut off from reality. We have become atrophied, isolated from our senses, from others, from the world.

For us, even an activity as sensorial as meditating has become a *fully conscious* act, which we hold in highest esteem. It is a reflexive action, purely spiritual, independent from any other reality. I must admit that for many years, this description of med-

itation as becoming "conscious" didn't shock me; I even used it
myself, until I finally grasped the misunderstanding it leads to.
We naturally associate consciousness with reflection, consciousness with intellectual exercise, consciousness with knowledge,
consciousness with control. However, meditation is not geared
toward the mind alone, but to our entire being. It has little to do
with this discrete, abstract form of consciousness as it has been
understood since the seventeenth century. Rather, it's there to
deliver us from it!

This is because meditation does not consist in being *conscious*, but in reaching a feeling of presence with the entirety of
our being—our body, our heart, our emotions, and our mind—
as it is anchored in the world. Meditating does not mean reflect-
ing, but feeling. It means being present to what is happening,
quite simply, without constantly trying to be conscious of what
this might lead to. It's like how cyclists keep balance on their
bikes without thinking; they don't think consciously about the
ideal angle for the bike in order to avoid falling over on one side,
they just trust themselves. They leave themselves behind, uncon-
cerned, without thinking about the way they pedal or the way
they hold the handlebar or the configuration of the road. Nor do
tennis players, on hitting an opponent's shot, calculate the angle of the racket or the speed of the ball; if they manage to hit it
back, it is because they have forgotten themselves and become
one with their movements and the situation, by being present—
not by being conscious.

Becoming conscious, as the term has been understood
since Descartes, means preventing yourself from coinciding

with life and watching yourself get on with it. On the other hand, meditating means coinciding with life. This does not involve being conscious, but open. For these reasons, I now stand against the command to be *conscious*. And in order to be as accurate and precise as possible in my presentation, I call the meditation that I teach *full presence*, rather than *full consciousness*. The point is not to create a distance from things in order to grasp them but, on the contrary, to try to engage with them and include them in our sense of being. Meditating involves freeing ourselves from the hell of total consciousness, to live in full presence with the entirety of our being, our sensations, our heart, our skin, our breathing, all while putting ourselves into the very flesh of the world—the water, air, trees, or sounds.

This is neither a revolution nor an innovation, but involves going back to the source. For, in Sanskrit and in most Asian languages, the basic practice of meditation is called *bhavana*, or "being in a certain way"—just like nature, which exists with no reasons or explanations. Here, meditation is understood as a deployment, letting what exists come to you, while being fully present. By introducing the notion of consciousness, we have reduced meditation to a mere technique, a cerebral exercise that activates a specific zone of the cortex, while putting other areas to sleep. We focus on its measurable effects on our neurons, but we forget that it concerns far more than just neurons; it involves the totality of our existence.

By theorizing meditation, we turn ourselves back into cerebral cortexes filling in charts and numbers, into businessmen such as the one the Little Prince met on the fourth planet. But if a businessman is present, and not just conscious, if he steps out of his personal control tower, checking everything from a distance, and allows himself to express his feelings, his instinct, his sensations, then he will become human again, and thus even more aware. He will carry out his tasks even more effectively, because he will be open, attentive, and present to reality, able to take the high ground and grasp situations in their entirety.

In this sense, meditation is not just a technique. It's a total overhaul of our way of being. In the English-speaking world the term *bhavana* has been translated by a different, far more appropriate term: *mindfulness*. The mind is not consciousness. It is both the brain and the fact of paying attention. It is an attentive spirit. "Mind the gap," as they say on the Tube in London. In other words, remain present so you can see and avoid falling. Be attentive rather than conscious, and progress confidently through life. We are not attentive if we remain wrapped up in ourselves; instead, we must be with whatever interests us. We must *be* in the world. The more attentive I am, the more present I am, and the more present I am, the more attentive I become. Attention and presence help one other mutually, and thus stand as the deepest source of meditation.

Meditating opens us up to a different relationship with time, space, ourselves, and the world, to which we are then fully connected, instead of being isolated in the fortress of our consciousness. This attitude should lie at the basis of our entire existence. Do I really need to be conscious that I'm holding a glass of water and am about to raise it to my lips? Isn't it enough that I am present to my glass of water, can feel its coolness first in my hand and then between my lips? The trap of consciousness is a constant danger. It's that reflexive push that makes me double up everything I do—I eat, and I watch myself eating. I try to grasp and control everything. What a suffocating way to live!

We count our steps when we walk, we measure our speed when we run, comparing it all to yesterday's performance. We intellectualize what we have on our plates as we eat rather than letting ourselves go so that we can taste it, savor it with our senses, attend to the sensation of hunger or satiety inside us. We wave to a neighbor after thinking about it and deciding to do so, as if this relationship with others was not primordial to human existence. By being conscious, we forget to be present. By thinking, we forget to be delighted. Our initial reflex is to take distance. Even in the practice of meditation, I remain at a distance to control my respiration, my thoughts, and my breath. And by being so self-conscious, by placing myself in the center of a web, I forget about presence.

Meditation, hypnosis, and psychoanalysis liberate us from the artificial ideology of consciousness and from its crushing grip. They are there to remind us that a human is above all a living being who feels, has sensations and emotions, and is run through with experience that is far more complex than what the screen of consciousness restricts us to.

By wanting to check everything, we terrorize ourselves. When we accept the idea of opening ourselves up to sensorial perceptions, the universe reveals itself in its hugeness. We can then, in the words of William Blake, "see a World in a Grain of Sand."[5]

Hearing birdsong is not just hearing a sound. But to find it, we must be present.

8

STOP WANTING TO
BE PERFECT

Accept life's storm

*Impose your luck, embrace your happiness and
go toward your risks: by looking at you, they'll
get used to it.*

—René Char, *The Dawn Breakers*[1]

When I started meditating twenty-five years ago, my goal was to become less vulnerable, less shy, less complicated, less impatient, calmer, more confident, more solid, and more relaxed. I had assembled everything I didn't like about myself and wanted to change, along with everything I did like about myself (not much) and wanted to bring out more. My list was longer than my arm, and it painted the portrait of the person I wanted to become. He wasn't much like me. He was perfect, and likable at last, or so I thought. At the time, I felt sure that other people were perfect, or at least far closer to perfection than I was. In my own eyes, I represented a very large number of failings and weaknesses.

We want to be perfect because we refuse failure, which we view as disastrous and humiliating, the end of a journey, be it professional or sentimental. We have been brought up to forget that in real life, failure is not only inevitable but also necessary. It is what makes us grow. We do not learn to fail, we fail to learn. Children who refuse to fall will not learn to walk. If they get upset because they've gone over the line while coloring, then they'll never learn to color properly and coordinate their movements. Some cultures value mistakes; some people even go so far as to include them in their résumés. They are proof that we have tried, even if we haven't succeeded. They show that we wanted to go further and embrace life.

As a student, I was considered a failure. The only reason I passed each grade was my father's ability to convince my teachers that I was finally going to get to work the following year. But things didn't turn out that badly. I graduated high school, went to college, and the challenges along the way didn't stop me from getting a PhD in philosophy.

We reject the idea of falling, of going off track, of straying from our goals. And yet: By the end of the nineteenth century, Thomas Edison had invented the lightbulb (and thus electric lighting), among many other things (over the span of his life, he patented 1,093 ideas). During that time, Edison admitted he had tried over nine thousand experiments that had failed; a friend said to him, "Isn't it a shame that with the tremendous amount of work you have done you haven't been able to get any results?" To which Edison replied, quite seriously, "Results! Why, man, I have gotten a lot of results! I know several thousand things that won't work."[2] Luckily for us, he wasn't someone who saw things as all or nothing, or who would be paralyzed by his failures, which were even more numerous than his discoveries. So why do we then expect ourselves to succeed perfectly and immediately? Why do we feel embarrassed whenever we fail? Why is failure so shameful?

It took me a while to become aware of how paralyzing the fear of failure can be—I quite simply couldn't take a risk or start a new project knowing that I might fail. About fifteen years ago, I'd already written a few books when I was asked to take part in a program about Buddhism called *Voix Bouddhistes* (*Buddhist Voices*)[3] on national television. I was absolutely terrified. Speaking about meditation on TV seemed so important, so serious, that I couldn't sleep. Racked with fear, I agreed to do it. And when D-day rolled around, I gulped down most of a bottle of whiskey before arriving for the show, even though I almost never drink. I wanted to be perfect, and thankfully the TV host's incredible kindness and intelligence allowed me to simply be myself. What a beautiful lesson in life! Because in the end, I can't be anyone but the person I am. With that in mind, what seemed to be most off-putting about myself gradually started to seem like a kind of gift I had to learn to accept.

We strive to be perfect, untainted by any emotional outbursts, and especially pain. We're ashamed to admit, even to ourselves, that we experience desire, anger, or disappointment. And if we do encounter these feelings, then we think that we can't "really" be happy—in our dualist, binary conceptions, this "really" is key: Either we're "really happy" or we aren't happy at all. But negating our painful (or negative) emotions, and resenting feeling or expressing them, essentially entails refusing a part of our humanity, which is made up not just of joy but also of sorrow, imperfection, distress, and dark moments. In the words of the Buddhist master Jack Kornfield, who has been an expert on mindfulness for almost forty years, we should distrust anyone who shows no emotion, who is never sad, unhappy, or angry: Such people are either psychopaths or dead.

Strangely, we're ashamed to cry in public, but we are moved when others dare to express their emotions. We're shaken up when we see a colleague, worn down by stress and fatigue, burst into tears: We don't judge; we comfort them wholeheartedly, with neither scorn nor pity. I remember during the 2016 Cannes Film Festival when the French actor Xavier Dolan teared up after receiving the Grand Prix. In his acceptance speech, voice trembling, he quoted the famous French poet Anatole France: "I have always preferred the folly of the passions to the wisdom of indifference."[4] He wasn't apologizing for crying, but in fact he was standing up for doing so.

Similarly, when someone confesses to a less-than-desirable past, we don't fault them for their mistakes; we appreciate their honesty. Robert Downey Jr. has openly discussed his wild upbringing, his stints in prison, his addiction to drugs and alcohol, and his relapses without placing the blame on anyone but himself. Who among us would dare to go so far in our confessions, with our heads held high, even around our closest friends? When we truly love someone, that includes their moments of emotion, their distress, and their fragility, which are part of their beauty as a human being! When it comes to others, we may admire their perfection but we don't love it, because it doesn't touch us. So why not learn this lesson when it comes to ourselves?

I often used to think that by daring to be imperfect in a world that values perfection, I was going be crushed or torn apart. About ten years ago, I was invited to give a talk at the Cathedral of Notre-Dame in Paris. On receiving this invitation, I thought of my four grandparents, who were all Polish Jews and victims of Nazism and anti-Semitism (they all lost family members in concentration camps): This was before the Second Vatican Council, at a time when, on Good Friday, Catholics would pray "also for the perfidious Jews." They would have been so proud to see me, a Jew, give a talk, standing in front of the altar, in such an important Christian site.

I carefully prepared my talk, weighing each word. But, at the crucial moment, I got caught up in the magic of the situation, and I completely let myself go. Many people have spoken to me since about what I said. They weren't struck by the logic behind my thought process, of which I was so proud, but instead by my emotion. This is the case every time. When we are most exposed, most genuine, when we don't cheat, only then do we find the possibility to truly connect with others. It's as if taking a risk is required for a real heart-to-heart connection. By trying to be perfect, we smother this precious source within.

Our obsession with perfection leads us to harass ourselves psychologically in a way that would be punishable by law if we did the same to someone else. We want so badly to be perfect that we no longer recognize our success, because we think that what we do is never enough. We constantly devalue ourselves by comparing ourselves to others. Have I just been promoted? Sure, but one of my colleagues is now in an even higher position, so he or she must be better than me. Did I bike five miles this morning? My brother rides eight every day. Have I just passed an exam? Yes, but it wasn't that hard. And so on!

The requirement to be perfect starts at school; we've all seen it on our report cards: "Room for improvement." I got that comment all too frequently, and it always led to frustration.

Twenty-five years later, I'm still not perfect. When it comes to meditation, nothing I planned turned out as I'd hoped. I've kept my flaws and my qualities, I'm still sensitive and vulnerable. But my relationship with these traits has changed completely. My violently aggressive attitude toward myself has faded. I've stopped wanting to be perfect. In truth, I couldn't care less. I still have lofty aspirations, but they steer clear of the cruelty of perfectionism.

I have undoubtedly disappointed a number of aspiring meditators by stating that meditation won't make them perfect. That meditating means accepting everything about themselves and burying the hatchet. Meditation is an act of benevolence toward ourselves, a profound yes. This is a deeply liberating approach within our society, dominated as it is by a perfectionist vision that has absolutely nothing to do with the reality of human existence.

I've certainly astonished many more who have asked me who meditation is aimed at, implying that only people with a calm, already meditative temperament (only people who are perfect, in a sense) could undertake this adventure. How wrong that is!

One of my neighbors was a talented architect and a man of great intelligence. Despite his cynical nature, I liked him a lot. Of course, he made fun of the fact that I meditated. For him, all that mattered was being strong and active; if he had a problem, he confronted it head-on. He viewed people with issues, anxiety, depression, or addictions as weak. He shrugged whenever I spoke to him about those who suffer from the violence inflicted by society, about suicide (which is a leading cause of death for young people around the world), or depression, which, according to the World Health Organization, is the leading cause of disability worldwide.[5] He refused to listen when I insisted on pointing out the inhumanity of our world. When I tried to explain that listening to yourself and giving yourself a break were not signs of weakness, the idea left him cold. He was so sure of himself.

When this independent man was diagnosed with cancer, he suddenly learned that he didn't have long to live, and after undergoing an operation, he hit rock bottom. I suggested he meditate with me, expecting him to turn down my offer. But, to my surprise, he agreed. And, every day for three months, I went to his place, where we would practice together for twenty minutes.

Within a few weeks, he had managed to make peace with himself and began to prepare his departure serenely. His family asked me how I had succeeded in transforming him. But I had done nothing; it was meditation that had allowed him to accept the unacceptable and embrace his fragility without fear. Despite his illness, the chemotherapy, and his imminent death, the man had become radiant.

But what is the point of meditating if you experience no changes in your moods, no matter the circumstances? If you're never sad, angry, unhappy, or burdened by insolvable problems? Of course, I don't know anyone who is immune to all the emotional vagaries that make up an existence. However, I do meet many people who are absolutely convinced they are the exception: They think everyone has a stable temperament apart from themselves. In reality, no one is perfect—if we see perfection as the immutable stability of a computer or, in the near future, of a robot. Such perfectionism is a denial of reality, a fiction we want to believe in, come what may. There is nothing human about this ideal we impose on ourselves (but not on other people). Nevertheless, we struggle to control our images, obsessed by the idea of concealing our slightest failings, the slightest wave, the slightest roughness, even during a storm. We use up an extraordinary amount of energy in doing so.

"Perfect" people, obsessed with goals, ignore reality to such an extent that they are often incapable of playing around with situations, of dancing with life. "The best possible" is not part of their vocabulary; only "the best" means anything to them. I have met perfectionist teachers whose goal is solely to complete the official curriculum. For them, textbooks should be taught through to the last page. If some students fail to keep up, too bad! Are they more effective than teachers who strive to teach as effectively as possible, while adapting themselves to the reality of a class, which is obviously never perfect?

Don't be perfect, be excellent! Excellence means reaching the summit of our humanity and savoring it, like the athletes of the first Olympic Games in Ancient Greece, whose motto was "Let the best man win." Today's athletes aim for perfection; winning doesn't suffice. They need to break a record. I remember Usain Bolt's victory at the 2009 World Championships in Athletics, in Berlin. He'd run one hundred meters quite magically, far ahead of his rivals. But the competition commentator cried out, "He's done it, he's done it, 9.58!" What mattered to him wasn't the splendor of the action, or the simple fact of winning, but "how much" the athlete had won by. During every Olympic Games, I am struck by how the commentators focus almost exclusively on the number of medals won rather than on the beauty of the events.

Don't be perfect, be ambitious! Accept your failings, ignorance, and imperfections. Just do your best, based on who you are, and on the reality you have in front of you. Don't cut yourself off from yourself, or from life.

Not giving a shit, in this sense, doesn't mean neglecting yourself, but instead accepting the world's complexity and nuances. It means accepting difficulties and hiccups, which perfectionists see as attacks on their success. It means no longer evaluating and controlling yourself all the time. It means to live, to enjoy life, and be enthusiastic. To leave behind anxiety and experience the stimulation of doing and living. Not giving a shit is based on a sense of confidence, and on being able to laugh at yourself.

Perfectionism also has an extreme and frightening side, called fundamentalism. Fundamentalists torture, sever, and destroy themselves while also destroying others, in order to live out what they call their faith in a way that seems absolutely perfect (according to their own criteria). Yet, whatever they do, however far they go, they never feel reassured, and endlessly feel the need to take it one step further. But this will never suffice: The more thresholds they cross, the worse they feel, and the more they need to pursue their growing folly while never deriving the slightest happiness from it. Such is the craziest rationale about the will to be perfect. This extreme example illustrates why perfectionists will never be perfect enough in their own eyes and too often spend their entire lives tormenting themselves in vain.

Don't take this path; instead, make peace with your distress and difficulties. In the meditation seminars I run, one of the most important points for me is to show the participants that what bothers them, or scares them, the things they'd like to eliminate from themselves, may, in fact, be positives.

A man named Charles started meditating with me many years ago and now runs the Western School of Meditation, which I founded. Initially, he often felt he was out of his league. He was unconsciously putting incredible amounts of pressure on himself, a pressure so strong that it stopped him from utilizing his own talents and taking risks. He was surprised when I didn't encourage him in his perfectionist endeavors; instead I simply suggested that he give himself a break. After that, he surprisingly (to himself) turned out to be the best at what he does...

9

STOP TRYING TO UNDER-STAND EVERYTHING

Discover the power of ignorance

Only learn with reservations. An entire life is not enough to unlearn what you naively, submissively, have allowed to be placed in your head—innocent one—without imagining the consequences.

—Henri Michaux, *Tent Posts*[1]

Acording to the laws of aerodynamics, the bumblebee can't fly, but the bumblebee doesn't know the laws of aerodynamics, so it goes ahead and flies," joked Igor Sikorsky, the Russo-American aviation pioneer and inventor of the helicopter, while developing the theory of what he called "the power of ignorance."[2]

We are severely lacking in this power of ignorance; we're

like bumblebees, but without the willingness to dare. We don't think of ignorance as power; we scorn it as the opposite of our supposed superiority as humans, our capacity to understand everything. If we were bumblebees, we would think first before taking flight. And we would likely never take off, given that it's impossible to fly. We would quite literally be prisoners of our own thinking, which would almost certainly get us killed.

We must be careful about this desire to understand everything: It can lead us astray. Should I change jobs, or companies, or where I live, if I realize that one or all of them have harmful effects on my life? When facing these serious questions, we tend to become lost in conjectures, calculations, and hesitations. We analyze the pros and cons again and again, letting months, then years go by, going back over our calculations and scaring ourselves into inaction, given that the "cons" column is never empty. In the end, we remain where we are, moping with regret ("Ah, if only I'd...").

We trail around these mounting regrets, accumulating sorrows, full of *If onlys*. We go to therapy in an attempt to understand, hoping that understanding will set us free. We may end up understanding many things, but that doesn't help us change. Many of us are capable of spending hours explaining our problems—issues with our parents, the wounds we've received—but then what? We become even more enclosed in ourselves than before.

My four grandparents narrowly escaped from the Holocaust. Their past was something we never talked about, and as a result it became all the more palpable and oppressive. In the early 1930s, one of my grandmothers had come to France on her own. When she started to hear about Nazi crimes in Poland, she did everything she could to go back, to warn her family and help them flee, but failed. Remorse stuck with her until the end of her life. In her living room, she kept a framed photo of her parents and brother, all of whom died in concentration camps. Her pain was unbearable, and she nurtured it every day by relentlessly replaying the story in her mind. When, as an adult, I finally managed to ask her about this, she answered in broken sentences, before sighing that she hadn't been able to tell them good-bye. I tried and tried to understand, persuaded that if I could simply comprehend why she hadn't been able to return to Poland, and how she might have succeeded, I'd be free and would automatically feel better. Isn't that what people are always telling us, from elementary school on? So I read books, I spoke with historians and psychologists, I interviewed witnesses and specialists. I almost became a specialist of the period myself; I knew plans and maps like the back of my hand; my head was crammed with facts, figures, and data, but the oppression was still there, along with my feeling of incompleteness. I kept on going nonetheless, immuring myself in this pain I'd inherited. I felt I had to succeed; I thought I needed to understand even more, because that's what society dictates.

I was afraid that if I lost control, a crack would open up, and my edifice would collapse, leaving me bare to the pain that was drowning me. I didn't want to put down the arms of reason, which I saw as a shield, nor did I want to abandon the rationale which, I still believed, would lead me to an answer. Stopping it all seemed almost suicidal!

As is often the case, I had to receive permission to stop. "To receive" implies a third party: a therapist, a confidant, someone who supports or loves us deeply and can give us the permission we need. Eventually, I let go of the rotten rope I'd been clutching and jumped, thinking I would fall into the void, whereas in reality I was finally heading toward life. I gradually gave myself a break, which is to say I saw that I could live with my pain and unanswered questions, that I could accept them as a challenge without looking for a solution. I learned to coincide with my own reality, as it was at that time. I accepted uncertainty.

I no longer tried to understand and instead engaged with my pain. Now I distrust people who claim to understand everything, even during the seminars I organize. Because when we think we know the answers, we tend to stop asking questions, discovering, and progressing. When we believe we hold the magic equation, we protect ourselves behind a theory and hang on to it. And so we miss out on reality, as it is embodied and experienced. "Understanding everything" is a terrible trap. It's terrible because though clarity can be necessary, it can also imprison us. Our existence is not a mathematical equation! Giving up on understanding everything is the only way to remain faithful to true human existence. It's the only way to give back to reality its breath, its rhythm, and its wholesome abundance.

By abandoning the desire to understand everything, we awaken a second force within: our intuition. Take, for instance, the following study that was administered to two groups of students, one German, the other American. They were all asked a single question: Which city, Detroit or Milwaukee, has the larger population? The American students, who were naturally better informed about their country's geography, thought about it, gathered data, and for the most part answered Milwaukee. The Germans, given that they had less information to go on, were forced to rely on their intuition. Most of them said Detroit, because it was the city they were more familiar with, and they were right.[3]

We rationalize our work, even when we sense instinctively that we're making a mistake. We're fascinated when other people come up with an idea, but we don't allow ourselves to abandon our usual processes to pursue one of our own. We even rationalize our personal lives: We all know men and women who look for the perfect partner using strategies essentially derived from marketing techniques. They rationalize their approach, intellectualize ways to increase their potential, barricade themselves against random events or the unknown, and become so focused on a specific goal that they lose the most important point: life. Years later, these men and women are still searching for the perfect partner.

The intuition I'm talking about has nothing esoteric about it. It's not some mysterious sixth sense, or a power reserved for the happy few. It shows up whenever we must make a snap decision, when we don't have enough time to gather all the information we need to proceed rationally. We then have two choices: either hesitate and dither, or make the leap. Despite what we might expect, we are not leaping into the unknown; we know far more than we think. We are constantly stocking up all kinds of knowledge through various channels—and not always the channels typically used to convey knowledge. While this information doesn't necessarily rise to the surface of our consciousness, it exists inside and forms a well of knowledge that our intuition uses to guide us. When I sense that a given solution to a problem is the right one, or that it will worsen a situation, I'm not staring into a crystal ball; I'm instantly analyzing the pointers and information that I often don't even know I possess.

In this respect, intuition isn't irrational. It can even be a form of underground rationality, something we can tap into more easily when give ourselves a break. When we stop our endless—and paralyzing—self-scrutiny, and instead agree to listen to ourselves. When we leave behind this dream of wanting to know and control everything, it allows us to shift to a different level of understanding. Can intuition lead to error? Of course it can, in the same way that our calculations, no matter how rational they are, don't always help us succeed!

But by cultivating our intuition and accepting that we won't understand everything, we awaken a third force within: creativity. Creativity isn't reserved for a handful of artists, nor is it a gift that only a few people possess. We all have it within. But we block it out, for one very simple reason: Being creative entails losing our reference points, thus allowing ourselves to change. And, naturally, we resist change, because we fear the unknown. We've decided that stasis is the safe, practical solution, and we've passed this down to our children by shaping them to fit a certain mold meant to help them enter the job market later on.

This solution doesn't make much sense for the twenty-first century: Our world is constantly changing. Today's training will be out-of-date tomorrow, when other skills and abilities will be required—skills that will be far easier to acquire if we've been brought up to be resilient, adapt, and adopt new paradigms. What's the point of reading a book like Homer's *Odyssey*? To help us be more human behind a ticket office window, more competent when managing a team, or more effective in moving from one software program to another. To be more aware of the complexity of a situation and its ramifications. In sum, to be creative, whether professionally or personally, or even simply when putting together a meal. Wittgenstein, the Viennese philosopher, thought that philosophical investigations were an "unsurpassable source of paradigms for learning something new about the world."[4] So are we ready to abandon our resistance to change and learn something new? Are we ready to be constantly disoriented, the better to take the leap? There lies the whole question of creativity.

I often compare this approach to learning to swim. We can practice on a stool, knowing perfectly well all the movements of each stroke, but diving into the water is a different story. Once in the water, we have to reinvent the movements we learned on land, otherwise we'll surely sink. Swimming is just like life, a gamble. Not giving a shit means throwing yourself into the water and opening up to the possibilities that will unleash your creativity. It means leaving behind any rigid framework and accepting that we don't know, we are not in control.

IO

STOP RATIONALIZING

Let things be

You should never open up the belly of the mystery.

—René Char[1]

To be more rational is, of course, a worthy ambition. Rationality is a way of emerging from superstitions and false beliefs, of not being ruled by our own subjectivity and emotions. It makes it possible to design a framework for living together. But our quest for rationality has also gotten out of hand.

Rationality today too often forgets to be reasonable, sometimes even playing *against* the demands of reason. We think of rationality as the solution to all our problems, trying to put everything in order and understand it all. In doing so, we've created a major handicap for ourselves, one that is even more paralyzing because we consider it a strength. It's hard for us to even recognize the madness that lies behind such an obsession.

The slightest decision or commitment must be backed up by the experts we listen to, with their knowledgeable arguments—but these experts so often get it all wrong. And that's because the basis of their thought is far too narrow. These technocrats make decisions that may well be thought out, but they're disconnected from reality, from the heart of life.

By wanting to calculate everything, they get stuck. Their reasoning seems logical, but it doesn't work. Why? These experts understand every aspect of a problem theoretically, but by reducing it to a set of numerical data, their understanding becomes abstract and inhumane. Up to their necks in numbers, they don't have time to get to know the actual problem. They stop asking themselves questions because they have all the answers. When they try to make reality (which is always more complex than our calculations) fit into a clearly defined framework of logical thought, they're forced to simplify. Thanks to their prestigious qualifications, no one doubts the basis of their arguments. But they commit a major error of reason: Calculating everything does not mean being able to think. How many times, obsessed with numbers and rationality, do they get things seriously wrong, because they haven't dared to lift their eyes from their charts? Then they claim they've been taken by surprise: by stock market crashes, by floods, shortages, or surpluses, by good or bad news. But never, ever, do we hear them admit: "I didn't know how to do this" or "I didn't understand."

I'm no more an enemy of figures than I am of rationality, so long as they don't conceal the complexity of reality. Instead, they should allow us to explore it, with the humility we all as human beings should have.

I'm not throwing stones at anyone—neither the experts nor the technocrats. After all, we all adopt this mode of thought to one degree or another. We insist that reality should fit into a column, even if we have to ram it in artificially, so that an intellectual construct can give us the illusion of being on the right track. We are the wise men whom the apostle Paul blamed for not understanding the essential before adding the following statement, which we should never forget: "the letter killeth, but the spirit giveth life" (2 Corinthians 3:6 KJV). The way we process is killing off life.

Rationality considers truth something to be understood, like a simple calculation. But there are many other ways to have a relationship with truth: through political life, ethics, art, or caring relationships. Limiting ourselves to rationality has wiped out the very basis of our shared humanity. In the name of rationality, we've set up mechanisms, methods, and protocols that have nothing to do with human reality. It's easy to understand why the rates of suicide, depression, chronic anxiety, and burnout are continuing to rise in Western countries. It is high time we realize this is not a "trend," as Didier Lombard, the former CEO of the French telecommunications company France Telecom, put it in 2009 when he discussed the wave of suicides among his company's employees.[2] Nor is it a psychological problem that concerns only a small minority. It is the brutality of the rationalization of a management that has no concern for the physical and mental health of its employees.

Not giving a shit means learning to kick our addiction to calculation and understanding the violence and radical dehumanization it implies. It means allowing a form of deeper intelligence to exist within us. This kind of intelligence isn't just formed in our brains (be it the left brain of reason, or the right brain of emotion); it also needs our senses, our bodies, our eyes, and our hearts if it is to exist. It needs reality and the world. It needs to take a step back for a wider perspective on human beings. Their well-being. Their accomplishments.

Let's be clear: I'm not declaring war on rationality. In fact, I think it's indispensable. Like anyone else, whenever I have a full day I try to organize it as well as possible, to rationalize my time and prepare my work. When I'm sick, I go see a doctor who follows a logical, rational course, based on facts. But I also insist on giving myself a break, in order to reengage with the enigma of existence. To understand what it means to be human, outside of all these diminishing orders and diktats.

This obsession with rationality is all the more terrifying in that it no longer really falls under reason, but under the dictatorship of efficiency. Rationality makes sure we all submit to the crushing power of efficiency.

I'm not declaring war on efficiency, either: In my own work, I try to be as efficient as possible. At the same time, I refuse to let it set the tone of my entire life. There are times when efficiency is marvelous, and times when it becomes insane, like how to look after my children, talk to a friend, or take an evening stroll in the garden. In those situations, there's no need for "progress reports," "clocking in," or "human resources." Let's manage our bank accounts, but not our emotions or our children. Let's control a company budget, but not its employees.

Meditation is now being used as part of this totalitarian rationalization. Meditating to be more efficient, more profitable, and forfeit your soul. Being aware of everything to better control it. To increase productivity. To dehumanize. So that it becomes all-encompassing and global.

Let's put a stop to this. Let's finally allow life to spring up in all of its effervescence.

II

STOP COMPARING

Base yourself on what you feel, even when you alone feel it.

—Henri Michaux, *Tent Posts*[1]

Most of us have been finding our place and measuring our progress by comparing ourselves with others since childhood. On the playground, we line up to see who's the tallest and strongest. Back in the day, you'd have to shoot a marble the farthest; now it's beating a level in a video game. In the classroom, we're encouraged to compare our grades and our abilities. As adolescents, we compare ourselves for reassurance. And now, as adults, we do so for comfort.

Comparison is a natural, human inclination. What's problematic is the paradoxical and consumerist command to be like everyone else—not to rock the boat—but at the same time, to be different. "Think different," as Apple's slogan goes, even though Apple sells millions of the same computers, tablets, and smartphones around the world. So be different, by doing the same thing as everyone else!

This paradoxical command is known to psychologists as a *double bind*: a constraint of two opposing injunctions which can lead to severe, long-term psychiatric problems. It is moral harassment, and this is what brand marketing, and twenty-first-century capitalism in general, has become. We convince ourselves we stand out from the crowd by buying this particular car, wearing these shoes, carrying this bag, or going to this restaurant. But all we're really doing is following the flock, contributing even more to the dictatorship of general uniformity. The worst part is we don't even realize we're becoming sheep: We're all about "thinking different," aren't we? Ironically, even the critique of capitalism itself has become a product of the troubling uniformity of modern capitalism.

Forced to think and act under this double bind, we no longer know what we want or desire, independent of the norm. I'm not trying to condemn, for some moral purpose, our tendency to compare ourselves, or to go with the flow. As I've said, it's only natural. The notion of comparing ourselves isn't detrimental in and of itself.

We each belong to small groups that have developed their own cultures—take, for example, sports team fans. We participate in such a group by sharing its references and vocabulary. We remain a part of this big family by adhering to its criteria, its ways of being, and even of dressing. One way or another, the group's culture takes over, a norm becomes imposed, and we must fit a certain mold. Otherwise, we run the risk of being excluded.

On a small scale, this exclusion isn't terribly problematic; we leave one small group, in which we took part for a precise activity at a specific time, to join another. But it becomes oppressive when we no longer feel able to leave. Without realizing, having lost any outside markers, we find ourselves prisoners of a suffocating mold. We stop asking ourselves questions, hesitating, or having doubts. Even when, deep down, a little voice says no, we shut it up and go with the flow. It's so much easier that way! Plus, we're afraid of being excluded, isolated, or rejected. This problem becomes especially critical when the suffocating mold is society as a whole.

To clarify, I don't consider myself a radical critic of consumerism. Being "anti" is just another kind of imprisonment. What we oppose, what we complain about, drains our freedom, our ability to pose questions and even to reinvent ourselves. Being anti just means always opposing. Instead, I aim for a more constructive vision—one with a closer hold on reality. I'm not so naïve as to think my approach can sweep away this underlying sheep mentality, but I do think it can help us find the courage to see the extent of the phenomenon, and thus acknowledge it more freely.

I don't reject society; instead, I refuse the way comparison pushes us to be uniform. I have the right to wear colorful clothes if they cheer me up, or to poke the hive, so to speak, even when the rules warn not to get too close. To be one of a kind, because we're *all* one of a kind, and to accept that my singularity is not something fixed but evolves every day, according to who I meet, what I read, and what I experience in life.

Who am I? I don't know—it's a constant rediscovery. I want to be free to compare myself and be myself, to follow the trend or stay out of it, to conform or be unique. Free to ask myself what I really want. Free so that I no longer struggle to smother my weaknesses and differences. Free to love myself, as Jean-Jacques Rousseau described it, when he criticized this obsession with comparing ourselves as a source of continual dissatisfaction: "Love of self (*amour de soi*), which regards only ourselves, is content when our true needs are satisfied. But self-love (*amour-propre*), which makes comparisons, is never content and never could be, because this sentiment, preferring ourselves to others, also demands others to prefer us to themselves, which is impossible. This is how the gentle and affectionate passions are born of *amour de soi*, and how the hateful and irascible passions are born of *amour-propre*."[2] The love of self he's talking about here is what I prefer to call benevolence toward yourself, or self-kindness, and it doesn't bear the same emotional charge as love. It goes hand in hand with the idea of not giving a shit: I stop judging myself, evaluating myself, comparing myself, having to be like this or like that.

Deep down, we envy those who dare to break free from the mold, but we hesitate before taking the plunge ourselves, because we're afraid, irrationally, of being rejected, ending up alone and isolated from others. It's the fear of not being accepted because we aren't like everyone else—the fear of being different and of the unknowns we'll face if we embrace those differences.

When I was younger, I was afraid that if I embraced who I really was, the small group I belonged to would see it as a betrayal. My parents wanted me to work for the family business, a small clothing company. I really didn't want to. They also wanted me to go to a good school, get married, and have kids. I haven't done any of those things. Instead, I took up meditation. At first, they thought I'd joined a cult and they even tried to contact the police about it. But I had found my way—the one that spoke to me and enthused me. I couldn't care less about the "good career" they wanted for me. Sure, I wasn't rolling in it; for years, I did a series of odd jobs and lived from paycheck to paycheck. But I had enough to eat, and that was enough for me, because I was living out a great adventure. I was happy.

Of course, I was still afraid of being a disappointment. No one got what I was doing. At the time, meditation seemed so strange! I simply faced my fear, unashamed. As I became more conscious of it, the fear stopped manipulating me; it slowly allowed itself to be tamed.

When you leave the flock, you may undergo a certain amount of solitude. But it's a full and healthy solitude, not isolation. I have mastered my solitude and have now befriended it. At the beginning, I was afraid of it and avoided it at all costs. I sought comfort in the social whirl, considering solitude a waste of time. Then, despite my apprehension, I tested it out. I looked it in the face, became familiar with it, and now I regularly take a few hours or days to get back in touch with it. Sometimes, in order to reconnect with myself, I spend a few hours activity free: I don't pick up a book, I don't watch a film, I don't tidy my apartment. I open my inner doors and windows and let the richness of these hours come to me. I inhabit my solitude and start to hear it again. I weave a genuine bond with myself and let the things I didn't know—or which I generally try to ignore—reveal themselves to me. I'm in communion with myself, with others, and with the world.

Is this difficult? We've all experienced a solitude that's relaxing and soothing: when we're walking alone in nature, when we stop the clock for an afternoon on vacation and spend it on a hammock, when we emerge from our everyday routine and realize we're okay. My solitary interludes are nothing more than that. It is an incredibly full solitude, because it consists of me communing with my own existence.

Unlearning the habits we've learned since childhood and that prevent us from being ourselves will take more than a few weeks or months. It's the work of a lifetime, and it's a work destined to stay unfinished: In the end, I'll always remain an enigma to myself, to my relationship with the world, and to others. The path toward one's self isn't laid out like a road map. It's an adventure. Whatever the numerous books on the subject may say, there are no predetermined steps. The classic routes of introspection are illusory. Being you doesn't mean defining yourself; it's not something you can do by simply taking a personality test or seeing a psychologist. It doesn't mean studying yourself; it means forgetting yourself.

When you look deep into yourself, you're sure to get lost. I appreciate the author Georges Bernanos's remark, in the preface to *A Diary of My Times*: "Knowing yourself is an itch that imbeciles scratch."[3] Knowing yourself is the fruit of a process that would ideally start in elementary school, with teachers attentive to each child's singularity. It would continue into adolescence, when each young person would be encouraged to find the spark of joy that excites them—when they find a task they're happy to accomplish, for the tasks that fulfill us are the ones we do best. But we aren't taught about the link between joy and success...on the contrary, we're told success will make us happy. But what does success mean? Getting good grades, a good job, a nice car? Bullshit!

When we're happy with what we're doing, we succeed: This is a major shift in perspective. By not giving a shit, we discover inner resources we didn't know we had. If we take a moment and don't do anything at all—if we give in to a situation and simply go with the flow—we may be surprised to discover riches we didn't know existed.

Schools have set up various forms of counseling centers that welcome teenagers with the all-too-frequent question: "What do you want to be when you grow up?" But how can teenagers know that? How can they know what appeals to them before experiencing the actual situations? Before opening their eyes to the world and letting themselves be guided by their own aspirations? What's more, are they given the opportunity to wander off down a new path? To avoid the crowded highways and choose their own way? It may be a winding path, but if it's the way that truly suits them they will follow it passionately. By comparing ourselves to others, we no longer dare to find out what we really want, what appeals to us, what interests us, what we genuinely desire to do. We are stuck in a rigid, fossilized idea of our identity.

Could Paul Cézanne, the founder of modern art, have existed if he'd refused to listen to himself? His ambition was to paint in the style of Nicolas Poussin, the great seventeenth-century classic master. He failed. He could have put away his brushes and done something else with his life, but he preferred to stick to what appealed to him and do his best. His aim was not to be different or original but, more prosaically, to restore life in painting by relying on his own direct experience of his subjects. Every year, the salon where artists exhibited their work turned him down, but Cézanne persevered. When Émile Zola, his childhood friend, criticized him for not taking enough care in depicting his subjects, Cézanne severed ties without hesitation. Art critics couldn't understand his obsession with working in great volume rather than great detail. Fortunately, Cézanne continued down his own path. Not trying to revolutionize art, but just trusting his hand as it held the brush. Letting his intuition speak to him.

Cézanne didn't become Cézanne by studying the depths of his soul, but rather by forgetting himself. By following his own path. By doing the best he could. By starting all over, again and again. By looking at Mont Sainte-Victoire, or a few apples on a table, or his wife sitting on a chair. He was constantly dissatisfied and animated by an ever greater and deeper desire to liberate reality even more. It was the challenge of painting that mattered to him, not his moods.

Being you is not an egocentric affirmation of individuality. Nor is it an affirmation of your singularity, excluding all else. We are, as Aristotle pointed out, relational, political beings. Being yourself means discovering bonds, obligations, and commitments.

When I started to meditate, my mother said to me, in annoyance at my perseverance: "I don't understand why you spend all that time navel-gazing." But meditating doesn't involve navel-gazing or looking deep inside; it means paying attention to the reality that calls out to us, grasping it just as it is. It means forgetting yourself to open out to the world. And letting yourself be.

One of the meditation cycles I teach focuses on confidence. To stop comparing yourself to others requires confidence! But by that, I don't mean self-confidence or self-esteem. Personally, I have no confidence in what I call "me." I have confidence in the profoundness of meditation, because I have seen its fruits. When I speak, I have confidence in what I'm saying, because I've experienced it.

Real confidence, as I like to teach it, is unconditional. It is a confidence in nothing, in my humanity, in the humanity in me that knows better than I do. A confidence in life, which will allow me to discover resources right at the heart of any given situation. It is a confidence far more radical than self-confidence. It is a state of mind that allows me to root my presence in the world. And, finally, to be.

12

STOP BEING ASHAMED

Be vulnerable

If you want to be original, be human; no one else is anymore!

—Max Jacob[1]

At age eleven, innocent love was rather complicated for me: I would fall for boys who, like nearly all the boys on the playground, liked girls. I was twelve when, alone on the playground one day, I started screaming. I was screaming because I couldn't take the harshness of this world any longer, a world in which I felt like an alien.

My sole ray of sunshine was the feelings I had for a classmate. I had a crush on him, and one day confided in him that I wasn't interested in girls. I didn't say anything else after that. We just stared at each other for a while, and I felt like I could trust him.

Sure enough, he continued to prefer girls, but he didn't reject me: We remained friends.

I couldn't do the same with everyone. With my parents, it was a game of deception. I sensed that my homosexuality would be a disaster for them. In truth, they were terrified of it, and sometimes mentioned the subject at the dinner table as if it were a disease, a pathological monstrosity. I was scared of shocking them. At the same time, I couldn't really see the problem: Being in love is one of life's most beautiful experiences! I learned not to talk about my feelings, but I continued to love, and each time I was dazzled: When we love, we are caught up in light, we leave ourselves behind to meet someone else, and we become alive.

When I was twenty, I ran into my former classmate by chance. We reminisced about the scene on the playground, and he told me he knew I had a crush on him. He knew it, but he'd remained my friend. He'd been struck by my courage to speak so directly and my willingness to trust him. From that day on, I began to accept the fact that I was vulnerable, fragile, overly sensitive. I no longer tried to conceal my tears when they filled my eyes. I no longer tried to harden myself from the fear of being beaten up. And I started laughing at the proverb that claims, "The heart sinks or swims..."

When we've been beaten, wounded, or betrayed, we try to harden. We decide we're not going to open ourselves up anymore. But this is like throwing out the baby with the bathwater, and it denies a part of our humanity. There is another path: finding the strength not to harden.

"To toughen up and to harden ourselves are two different

things. We confuse a lot of things in times like these.... I think I'm toughening up each day, but I will likely never harden," wrote Etty Hillesum in her *Diaries* in 1942.[2] Toughening up involves finding a kind of solidity so we can go on taking risks, loving, being amazed, and hoping. Hardening ourselves means putting concrete walls around our hearts and shutting ourselves up so much that we miss out on life. It means refusing the inherent fragility of our humanity. It means refusing to be human and becoming the very shell we hide behind, lacking confidence in ourselves, in life, and thus automatically cutting ourselves off from everything around us.

Moved by the fragility of a rose, and fearing that it would catch a cold or be attacked, Saint-Exupéry's Little Prince watered it and then sheltered it under a globe. Once protected, the rose tormented him with its constant whims until the day of his departure, when, with its heart now open, it admitted that it had been foolish and told him: "I need to put up with two or three caterpillars if I want to get to know the butterflies. Apparently they're very beautiful. Otherwise who will visit me? You'll be far away. As for the big animals, I'm not afraid of them. I have my own claws."[3]

Let's be clear: Accepting your weaknesses doesn't mean breaking down in tears all the time, or abandoning your claws when "large animals" draw near. Allowing yourself to be sensitive doesn't imply letting yourself sink beneath the weight of the world's suffering. It means allowing yourself to be shaken, moved, horrified, and angry at injustice, unhappiness, and evil.

Being vulnerable is not a weakness: It is a marvelous capacity to be touched. But we're ashamed of it. Shame is the social face of guilt; we feel guilty about being how we are, so we torture ourselves trying to be "better," poisoning our own lives. Deep down, what do I have to feel guilty about?

"We shouldn't console ourselves. The truth is to be inconsolable and happy," wrote the Belgian psychoanalyst and writer Henry Bauchau, quite rightly.[4] Inconsolable about all the sorrows—our own and the world's. Being inconsolable means making peace with our wounds and opening up to the possibility of deep, real happiness, which is quite different and far more beautiful than the caricature of happiness so widely vaunted today, in which we've overcome our faults. Does "feeling good" mean being smooth and making no waves? Nonsense! Who among us doesn't have weaknesses? So long as we consider them as such, they will continue to be weaknesses, even handicaps. If we agree to embrace them, accept them, and even love them, they transform into strengths that help us progress. "Feeling good" means feeling good about everything we are.

The practice of meditation, sitting with your back firm, your chest tender and open, expresses the attitude I've adopted to life. I've acquired strength, yet I feel tenderness. I do sometimes cry, but I don't let it bother me; something inside me stands up beyond my tears. Having this experience tells me there's something I need to listen to.

This is what I call the third way: neither rejecting your vulnerability nor being crushed by it. It's a method of looking at and living out your emotions with gentleness and humor. Of recognizing and admitting them, and thereby preventing them from taking over. If you're sad or moved, don't be ashamed to say so or to live it out. It's vain to think we could suppress all our emotions, as though we control everything we feel. How pretentious!

When I started to accept my own fragility, I discovered something I hadn't seen while I was too busy putting up my walls: I'm not the only person who's sensitive and vulnerable. We all are, to various degrees, and we hide it to a greater or lesser extent because we're ashamed. We see our fragility as a flaw, or the result of some trauma or lack of love we try to fish up by rummaging around in our past. I used to do this myself, blaming what I took to be a failing on my absentee parents, who both worked extremely hard, at all hours, even on weekends, and never took vacations. I analyzed myself and made my accusations, until I finally understood that fragility is inherent to humanity. It is the dignity of the human heart.

Let's get rid of the idea that superheroes made of steel really exist, and that we're just not one of them. There was once a time when superheroes themselves accepted their weaknesses. They even showed their humanity. Achilles, the hero of the Trojan War, was struck with a completely unreasonable rage, but his passion made him a renowned Greek hero. Lancelot was in love with King Arthur's wife, but this didn't stop him from being a pure-hearted knight, ready to confront both danger and convention. Percival was a rough, rather crude young man, but his innocence meant that he was free from making petty calculations and devising narrow strategies, and so he vanquished with elegance.

Too many of our contemporary heroes have no flaws or

weaknesses. Iron Man and Robocop, for example, give us the image of a heroism devoid of any human dimension. What's more, they're heroes because they're "ruthless machines," rather than humans. The type of heroism that used to consist of allowing our full humanity to blossom has now been reduced to its total absence. The message this sends is to cut out our "shameful" vulnerability.

Fortunately, despite this message, we still have our humanistic heroes, such as a tearful fireman who has just saved a child from a burning house. It's not so much his bravery that moves us as it is his displaying a moment of "weakness," which reveals to us some of our own stifled humanity. So why, then, do we obstinately reject in ourselves what we actually admire in other people? Amid the flames, the fireman revealed a strength he may not even have known he had. He comes out tougher, but not hardened. He has allowed himself to express the fragility we suppress. Looking out from behind our protective shells, we recognize this as a form of greatness.

Twenty-five years of meditation have helped me admit that my differences, my struggles, are not a big to-do, and there's no reason to turn them into one. I no longer feel obliged to put myself in a clearly marked box, and I'm proud to live in a country where, despite the pressure I've described, I can largely live as I want—and love who I want.

People often ask me how to overcome the shame of vulnerability. My honest answer is that there is no magical solution. I have no clearly laid-out plan promising to teach you to accept yourself if you simply follow the steps.

That would go against the very meaning of what I've learned. But what I can offer is the example of the path followed by those who have practiced with me over the past fifteen years. Each at their own rhythm, with their own experiences, failures, fears, and sometimes terrors. I've seen them each open up to the joy of being who they are—of not giving a shit, at least for a moment. I've watched as they've come to realize that meditation is not a technique with a list of rules to follow. It's not meant to make us more efficient, stronger, greater, or more independent. I've watched as they've come to accept the uncertainties in life, to take risks, dare to be who they are, and cast off fear. I've watched as they've learned to exist.

Going through this practice of meditation frees us from a good deal of useless armor and dead weight. For this reason, it's not always very comfortable, but it is always liberating. It's liberating precisely because it does not put us into a mold. It asks nothing of us. It opens up a space where we are allowed not to give a shit. I have no idea if you should meditate every day or twice a week. All I know is that mediation is a lost cause if it's turned into another to-do list item in your life. It doesn't really matter if you can't meditate every day. Or if sometimes you sit down, but then you get right back up. Don't try to make this into a challenge, or something you have to achieve. You can't learn to be free, but you can let yourself be free. It's there waiting for you; it just takes some time to accept it.

13

STOP TORMENTING
YOURSELF

Become your own best friend

*Perhaps everything terrifying is at bottom the
helplessness that seeks our help.*
>   —Rainer Maria Rilke[1]

I'm such an idiot!"

I heard these words in the Paris metro a few years ago,
but it could have been anywhere, anytime. A woman, deep
in thought, had just missed her stop. What she yelled out isn't so
different from what we whisper to ourselves all day long, like a
mantra in various forms: "It's not my thing"; "I'm out of my
league"; "I'm crap"; "I'm not even capable of..."; and so on.

We are our own worst critics. An insidious little voice inside
us, one we're hardly even aware of, constantly comments on our
thoughts and actions with a severity we'd never use on anyone

else, and with a partiality and persistence that's so critical, it's practically harassment. Out of habit, we no longer pay any attention to this voice, but it's there, rapping our knuckles, torturing us, belittling us. Its plan to undermine us works very well. You want proof? We constantly feel we have to apologize. For example, we start our conversations, letters, or e-mails: "I'm sorry," "Excuse me," "Pardon me," "I might be disturbing you, but..." Which all comes down to saying: "I know I'm pretty worthless in your eyes."

T. S. Eliot perfectly described this hell we so easily dive right into in his play *The Elder Statesman*:

> *What is this self inside us, this silent observer,*
> *Severe and speechless critic, who can terrorize us*
> *And urge us on to futile activity,*
> *And in the end, judge us still more severely*
> *For the errors into which his own reproaches drove us?* [2]

We observe and judge ourselves to no end. At some point, we fail. And then we have even more reason to look down on ourselves. It's a vicious cycle, with no exit. We must learn to tune out the intense cruelty of this self inside us, even if only for a moment.

Sometimes when we try to rise above this voice, we end up shifting to a higher gear of harassment. We up the ante, so to speak, against ourselves: "I was stupid to believe this wouldn't work out"; "How stupid I was to think I'm stupid..." We sink into the swamp we've created, we snare ourselves in our own nets, and these self-fulfilling prophesies stop us from progressing—like a child who's been told over and over again that they're no good at something, who ends up believing it and loses the will or desire to do better.

It's rare that we dare to congratulate ourselves, and if we do, we qualify it carefully: "For once, I've succeeded"; "How did I manage to do that?"; "Amazing, I've won!"

I grew up in France, where we've been raised with the old educational method that says if you tell a child they're beautiful, they'll become insufferable. That a student must hand in a completely flawless paper to get an A; otherwise they'd just rest on their laurels. So now when a member of our team closes a complex project, we don't congratulate them, because we think they'll stop trying, or they'll ask for a raise or even a promotion.

And this isn't just a French phenomenon—in cultures all around the world, we've convinced ourselves that progress can be made only by maintaining underlying pressure on individuals and on society as a whole. What a mistake! Less harsh educational methods have shown that when we help children recognize their positive qualities, they can unwind and find the necessary inner resources to do better.

By criticizing and never daring to congratulate, we undermine ourselves and those around us. And we end up truly believing in our inability to achieve, stifling our inner strength. Michel de Montaigne was right when he said: "To say less of yourself than is true is stupidity, not modesty."[3]

I know this all too well. For the longest time, I used to beat myself up, in particular for my lack of patience. Unsurprisingly, this didn't make me *more* patient; it just made me feel worse about it. Hearing that woman on the Paris metro say, "I'm such an idiot!" was a catalyst for me. I realized how harsh and tyrannical I was toward myself. I understood that what we see as normal is in fact a form of violence—I forgot my umbrella: how stupid! I mismanaged my schedule: how incompetent! I left my phone on silent: how foolish! I didn't run fast enough to make my train (even though there's another one two minutes later): how lazy! And I began to feel a certain softness for the person inside me who was constantly being belittled, a hint of benevolence toward this "me" whom I ordered around and constantly criticized.

Simply observe yourself on a daily basis, and you'll realize just how severe this self-harassment is. At that point, you'll be ready to find a solution to release yourself from this toxic environment. The first step is to count the number of times you belittle or insult yourself in a single day.

The second step requires you to treat yourself just as you would treat a good friend. In other words, with far more kindness than you typically offer yourself. The point is not to fawn over yourself by gazing in the mirror for hours at a time, and not to pay yourself endless compliments, but instead to have a gentle, generous attitude. *To let yourself be.* When a friend messes up, we simply tell them—we don't chastise them harshly about it, and we don't repeat ten times how unfortunate that slipup was. We talk to them about how to fix things, and about possible ways to avoid making the same mistake again. We don't make them feel guilty for the rest of their lives, or repeat "you should have" ad nauseam. We congratulate them when they deserve it, soothe them when they've failed, and help them heal when they're hurt. We don't endlessly blame them for their shortcomings. In the end, we *like* them, despite their flaws—and sometimes even because of them!

This is the attitude to adopt when becoming your own best friend. But this second step is generally misunderstood. We think being gentle and giving means being kind to ourselves in a naïve sort of way: congratulating or comforting ourselves narcissistically, like buying a dress or eating chocolate to treat ourselves, as some personal-development gurus suggest. If I've forgotten my umbrella when a storm is imminent, it won't help to pat myself on the back or repeat that I love myself. We are of no more help to a child if we belittle them all the time than if we let them behave capriciously without the slightest reproach.

When we stop caring so much about how we're supposed to be, the harshness we show ourselves becomes clear. So I beat myself up all the time, just as I was brought up to beat myself up. This realization makes me smile and makes the beating up less drastic and severe. In fact, it becomes laughable.

It's as absurd as all those "I should have" lectures we give ourselves, hanging on to a past we can no longer change instead of focusing our energy on the present. That's right, I should have brought my umbrella, but I didn't. Is there really a point in beating myself up all day? It won't make my umbrella magically turn up. While I'm busy beating myself up, I don't even notice the umbrella seller I've just walked past.

The art of not giving a shit is more than something we learn; it's a mantra we need to repeat as soon as we start to slip back into the dark mechanisms that govern us. It counters the "I'm useless" mantra, which comes to us almost automatically, whatever the situation. I'm not useless; I'm no prodigy, either. I accept myself as I am, unconditionally, and from there I see how I can improve. Yes, I'm absentminded, impatient, and anxious. But by their acceptance, by laughing at myself, I become less absentminded, impatient, and anxious. The kindness I awaken in myself is the most effective remedy of all.

Becoming your own friend is a difficult task, because it means taking apart all the mechanisms ingrained in us. It isn't a matter of understanding: It doesn't really matter why I have it in for myself, or why I'm angry, I just know that I am. I don't try to analyze anything; I just learn to acknowledge reality. Nor do I try to assess myself: This would mean placing myself on a scale, and comparing myself to a norm that doesn't exist. All I need to do is look, gently and kindly, at what I'm experiencing and how I'm experiencing it.

In the Western world especially, we're prone to become victims of self-inflicted violence; we've become experts at making ourselves suffer. In fact, this is one of the main obstacles that has slowed meditation from entering the West: The first Eastern masters who came from India, Tibet, Vietnam, and Japan didn't realize how unkind Westerners can be to themselves. They didn't understand how difficult it is for us to become friends with ourselves, a more common attitude in their own cultures—though of course, they have other issues.

I often like to tell this incredible story: In the late 1980s, the Dalai Lama invited several Western meditation teachers to his home in Dharamsala, India. As usual, he started by asking them a question: What is their main obstacle when it comes to teaching meditation? They all agreed it was the harshness Westerners inflict on themselves. Here's where the story becomes surprising: The Dalai Lama quite simply couldn't grasp what they meant. The interpreter tried various ways of explaining the concept and in the end the Dalai Lama understood. He was flabbergasted. "But all human beings should know what kindness is!" he cried. For him, for the Buddhism he grew up in, compassion is essential—compassion for all living beings, ourselves included.

Admittedly, we start out with a handicap: our belief in the fundamental malevolence of mankind, which comes from the Biblical invention of Original Sin. Since the eighteenth century, this idea has been amplified by the myth of mankind as selfish and evil—a myth that lies at the heart of political thought (via Hobbes), economic thought (via Adam Smith), all forms of demographic thought (via Malthus), and psychoanalysis (via Freud). We're convinced we're bad people, and that we should criticize ourselves constantly to eradicate the evil within us. If we find it difficult to give ourselves a break, it's because we are afraid of trusting ourselves; and if we do give ourselves a break, we fear we may very well discover a monster within.

This belief is essentially our rule of thumb. We think everything is driven by selfishness, envy, and jealousy. And, above all, that we should never let ourselves go. As a result, we're blinded, incapable of seeing that alongside malevolence, there also lies within us a capacity for goodness and generosity. The other is not always out to get us. Such a hasty simplification of reality and of our complexity makes us defensive and causes us to undermine ourselves.

When I first discovered meditation, the emphasis was on showing compassion to others. Treating ourselves with kindness was, and still is, one of society's greatest taboos. Values such as learning to be less hard on ourselves, becoming our own friend, and not beating ourselves up and feeling guilty are considered egotistical, or a luxury. And yet, egoists' problem is not that they love themselves too much; it's that they don't love themselves enough. This lack of self-affection leads to emptiness and frustration, which they try to make up for by endlessly seeking satisfaction. Egoists are immature children who need other people to do what they can't do for themselves—in particular, making friends with themselves.

We start out with a handicap: our egos, which are both a poison and an instrument of self-torture. Or at least when it comes to the ego in the sense that we understand it when we utter such guilt-inducing statements as: "It's my ego," "You've got a big ego," or "He's stroking his ego."

That ego is not the ego of Western philosophy. It is not Descartes's *ego cogito*, "a thing that thinks: that is, a thing that doubts, affirms, denies, understands a few things, is ignorant of many things, is willing, is unwilling, and also which imagines and has sensory perceptions."[4] Descartes also refers to it as the "mind," "cognition," or "reason," and he believed it existed only through *cogitatio*, through doubt, thought, and self-questioning.

Nor is it the ego of Buddhism, which doesn't actually exist.

The term is used only to show that we have no need to identify ourselves with our temporary, relational identities. In other words, if there is a "me," it is only relational and relative. Our true being is not a mean, narrow, guilt-ridden ego that we should fear for the rest of our lives, but a non-ego!

The ego as it is understood in the West, however, is a kind of personal and psychological "me," a solidification of myself. A me that feels guilty about itself. Guilty before having said or done anything. Once, when I thanked a physiotherapist for the work she'd done, she replied: "It's thanks to the method I use, which I now like to teach. My trainees are excellent, too. But that's my ego talking..." I was aghast. Why did she need to justify herself, and apologize for the excellence of the method she used so well, and no doubt taught just as well? Why this gratuitous attack against herself?

We're very clumsy with ourselves. We think we're doing the right thing, but we're often just banging our heads against a wall. We imprison ourselves in the guilt-ridden bubble that comes along with the notion of an ego. We are like a man locked in a room: First he tries to leave the room through the window, but it's too high. He then tries the chimney, but it's too narrow. He feels desperate. And yet all he has to do is turn around, and he'll see that the door is still open. Not giving a shit means being able to turn around and leave your prison at once.

This terrible lack of kindness, which eats away at our lives and at society, has led me to practice and teach how to meditate on loving benevolence, alongside mindfulness and complete presence. They are two wings of the same bird. When I enter the present moment, when I'm fully available, open, and attentive to what is, this mindfulness contains tenderness, friendship, and care, a dimension of love that necessarily makes it kind.

Yet in our culture, which views being kind to oneself suspiciously, the practice of benevolent love (or loving benevolence) can sometimes lead to a great deal of reticence. We see it as egotistical even though, on the contrary, accepting yourself fully and feeling compassion for yourself, in spite of your faults and failures, is an act of heroism. By their acceptance, they become transformed. My impatience is not dissolved by meditation: It remains inside me, but it no longer dominates me. I can even laugh at it.

One of the best ways to take this high road to self-reconciliation, self-friendship, and peaceful self-opening to the world is the practice of benevolent love. In this form of meditation, we deliberately invoke benevolence toward ourselves by reliving a moment when we truly felt loved. If we look closely, we realize that it's not necessarily a moment of passionate love, but more often an episode which, when seen from the outside, may seem trivial. In my case, it was something that occurred when I was a teenager.

I was thirteen or fourteen. Like many adolescents, I felt rather ill at ease, an alien in a strange world. I was on vacation at my grandparents' house in a small village in the south of France. I was especially close with my grandfather, ever since the day he came into my room, found me drawing (my favorite hobby at the time), and examined my drawings with interest. This was a revelation for me. My parents, who let me buy as much paper and as many crayons as I wanted, never bothered to look at what I was doing, and when I was gone, they threw it all away while tidying up my room. While they didn't do it out of meanness, I still experienced it as an act of malice. But as soon as my grandfather took a look at my drawings, my own vision of them changed.

During this same vacation, I was taking a walk with my grandfather when I suddenly felt the need to hold his hand, as I did when I was a child. We walked on for a few meters, in silence. I was too old to be holding an adult's hand, and I then realized how incongruous the situation was. But I sensed that, thanks to this hand, I was at last allowed to be who I was. My grandfather took my hand tenderly. A soothing feeling ran through me.

For me, this experience remains an image of benevolence: my hand, wrapped in my grandfather's, for a few seconds. When I practice, I spend a few minutes remembering this moment and feeling its bounty. I allow myself to relive the relief I felt at that time. I try to feel the qualities of this experience, its warmth, openness, and relief, independently of its context. That's how I'm able to direct my own affection toward my loved ones and, more generally, the world. By developing an initial benevolence toward myself, I discover the surprising radicalness of loving benevolence, and then I spread it.

Only by recognizing my right to be who I really am can I recognize that same right in others, in humanity, in the world.

14

STOP WANTING TO LOVE

Be benevolent

Those that go searching for love
only make manifest their own lovelessness,
and the loveless never find love,
only the loving find love,
and they never have to seek for it.

—D. H. Lawrence[1]

My grandmother really loved me. At least, that's what she told me every time she saw me. I have no doubt she meant it. When she said "I love you," it was always followed by the same litany: She'd ask me to call her more often, not to forget to see my cousin and uncle who, according to her, loved me so much, and to catch up with her more regularly—which I did, good grandson that I was. I should also cut my hair and stop studying such useless things as philosophy. Her love was marvelous, but it was also tormenting, because it placed an enormous guilt on my shoulders. Because I failed in all my duties.

Without any ulterior motives or meanness, she would use that "if" which so often comes out of our mouths: "If you love me...wash your hands, be good, finish your homework, etc." She was giving me all her love, but I saw it as conditional. Deep down, she never saw who I was, but that didn't matter to her. Her love was deep, and she wanted the best for me—the best from her point of view.

I later understood that my grandmother had never managed to make peace with her own solitude. She wanted me to free her from this burden, but that was obviously impossible. Whatever I did, I couldn't satisfy her expectations.

In high school, there was a philosophy teacher I sometimes had coffee with. We were sitting outside at a café one day when I was suddenly struck by a revelation: This man was happy to spend time with me because I was who I was. In this way, he loved me deeply. But if I'd told him I was touched by the way he loved me, he wouldn't have understood. He wasn't thinking in terms of exchanging emotions; we were just happy to be together, that afternoon, on the terrace of a café.

We too often use the word *love* without any benevolence involved. But love is often shown without being stated: This is benevolence. The word *love* has become so clichéd that it's hard to use and gives rise to many misunderstandings. It even becomes terrifying. We repeat it all day long, until it conveys no real meaning. On the other hand, we hold it back when it begins to well up inside us. Then we see it as a pair of handcuffs; we fear it's not actually true, that we're being played for a fool, that we're being rejected, or stifled. Deep down, the relationships that don't immediately bring to mind the word *love* (such as my relationship with my philosophy teacher) are sometimes the most loving in the real sense of the term. Those are the people who are truly delighted that we are like we are, and they want us to remain the people we're meant to be.

Let's stop wanting to love and stop forcing ourselves to say "I love you" artificially, conditionally, or conventionally. Let's be benevolent. That is how love begins—when we feel we can really be ourselves, when we discover that we are more like ourselves when we're with this other person, and we want that person as he or she is. When we wake up to a new relationship with life. When we can let it be.

Love is difficult, because it's always a form of grace. Why do I love you? I could, of course, draw up a list of reasons, but it would say nothing about the real reason. Deep down, I have no idea why I love you, and that's why I do. I love you because you are who you are. It's your mere existence that fulfills me, soothes me, and delights me.

I love you because you are. This should delight you; instead it worries you. You have trouble accepting that there's nothing you have to do. Give yourself a break—this is all you need to be able to discover the art of love.

15

STOP DISCIPLINING
YOUR KIDS

Meditation isn't Ritalin

*One has knocked at all the doors which lead
nowhere, and then one stumbles without
knowing it on the only door through which one
can enter—which one might have sought in
vain for a hundred years.*

—Marcel Proust[1]

I was at a friend's house when her daughter, a bubbly pre-
teen, came home from school. She clearly had a thousand
things to tell her mother and didn't know where to begin.
She was jumping for joy and her pleasure was a delight to see.
My friend didn't let her go any further: "You need to meditate,"
she said. Her daughter yelled: "But I'm calm, mom!"

This take on meditation upset me. I would go so far as to

call it monstrous. Sometimes I get parents who come to me complaining about their children's bad temper, or what they see as an inability to concentrate. What they're basically asking me to do is spend a few sessions of meditation with their child and send them back good as gold. When I get these kinds of requests, I point out the violent nature of their approach: So what you're saying is you want a child who's been atrophied? The same one, but without the parts you can't handle or dislike? A custom-made child?

When children misbehave and we send them to their room to calm down, we assume that, once alone, they'll think about their behavior and realize their error. Of course, that's not what actually happens: Once alone, the child in question will focus on the injustice of the punishment. They'll regret their parents' attitude and actions rather than be sorry for their own behavior. From this perspective, the punishment will have been pointless; such children will continue to get worked up and their parents will continue to punish them. Asking them to meditate to calm down falls under the exact same rationale. First, meditation is not an introspective exercise. Second, making your children meditate is an aberration. You can't make people meditate; you meditate with them. Meditation is not a project to force upon your children, but a state of presence you can share with them, which opens up quite a different perspective on the practice.

Let me say this once and for all: The point of meditation is not to calm children, or adults for that matter. It's not there to stop them from being children. On the contrary, it's there to *allow* them to be children—to unwind, to live, and to be fulfilled at a time when we place an incredible amount of pressure on them, to the point where we no longer know what being a child even means.

A meditation session is not the equivalent of a dose of Ritalin. It is not calming, but it is soothing. We consider children to be calm when they meet our criteria for not causing disturbances; in other words, they play alone without interrupting our own peace and quiet. As for being soothed, it means tensions and conflicts no longer have any room to exist. Practicing this discipline does not entail putting children into a mold of "good behavior," it means inventing a better way to enter into a relationship with them as they are, good or not. It fosters within them a curiosity about the world around them, what is at the present time. Its sole aim is to allow them to be.

Recent research on the brains of children has shown the damage caused by the violence of everyday stress. Under the effects of stress, the neurons' development changes, interneuron connections are organized differently, and some of them can become atrophied or disappear entirely (for example, those dealing with the control of emotions, relational capacities, or empathy). The brain clams up, in a sense, as if from a regular use of psychotropic drugs. Physiologically, stress leads to stress, and violence causes violence. The demands and orders we rain down on our children are a form of violence and a huge source of stress.

Now that we know this, we no longer have the right to duck the challenge of inventing a new, more benevolent form of education—and meditation could very well be part of this revolution. Instead of considering our children as being "ours," and needing to satisfy "our" plans, let's view them as friends or guests, some-one we make an effort to form a connection with, free from prior judgment or preconceived notions, and full of benevolence. Af-ter all, we don't ask our guests to fit into our image or fulfill our plans.

In this case, giving ourselves a break, or not giving a shit, is not an invitation to become lax. Obviously, children need to grow up, learn, and obey rules: The absence of rules is as wor-rying as their accumulation. Helping them progress, kindly and respectfully, doesn't mean letting them get away with their every whim, not washing when they don't want to, or not doing their schoolwork when it bores them. But there is a different way to lead them into playing this game. Cutting things short and shut-ting them up in their bedroom isn't a solution. Nor is endlessly repeating "Don't do that." Being benevolent and respectful to your children is not a matter of being nice to them, or of torment-ing them, but of easing each situation so that it becomes a dance. By engaging with your children, you see things together, rather than on opposing sides. You provide the rules of the game, you explain what you expect from them and what society will expect later on. You help them confront their own life, rather than tor-turing them to fit your life. You understand better what speaks to them, what hurts and moves them. You see their reality, you can grasp and interact with it. You discern what's there, and under-stand it. Meditation is a form of love in which you allow them to be exactly who they are.

Encouraging children to meditate also means teaching them the real meaning of paying attention, which comes about when they're free of pressure or stress—from the Internet, a video game, an upcoming exam, or a sports competition, which, even though it may be friendly, is really all about winning.

Of course, certain challenges are necessary. I fully support the challenges faced by the French soccer star Antoine Griezmann, who chose to leave his family at the age of fourteen to live in Spain and fulfill his dream. But that was his choice—not the fruit of his parents' frustrated desires. For him, it was a way to blossom, not to be crushed.

By helping children master a certain kind of silence, meditation allows them to set off toward the discovery of another way of life, one in which there might be less excitement, but we are still just as alive. It has nothing to do with the idea of forbidding Internet access or video games, but with finding a continuum where being alive in different ways is the main thread.

Having taught meditation to children, I know that they immediately understand what I mean by it, even more easily than adults, because they haven't yet been impregnated with our ideologies and reflexes, and they aren't yet prisoners of the straitjackets our society straps us into. For them, meditation is a natural state. They know how not to give a shit and enter into a friendly relationship with themselves. They are not yet cut off from their bodies and sensations, as adults are. They are more trusting in their own experiences. When I ask them to sit down, and "go home" for a few minutes, they immediately understand what this simple gesture means.

I regularly organize meditation seminars, lasting one or two weeks, during which some parents bring their children. There are planned activities for the children, but every morning I ask them to practice with us for a few minutes—that's all they need. They enter into the tempo at once, whereas adults need some time before really getting there, greeting themselves, their body, their heart, and their thoughts. Pablo was one such child. The way he meditated was strikingly natural. He didn't try to take on a role or create a character for himself, he didn't take himself seriously, as some adults tend to, and he didn't at all have the impression of undertaking some kind of mystical-magical ritual. One morning, I asked him to take my place and meditate facing the group. His attitude expressed better than any amount of words the sole message that I wanted to deliver: Sit down and stop giving a shit.

Today, Pablo is ten years older. He doesn't meditate assiduously, but he does come back from time to time to practice with me. He recently wrote me this e-mail, which I have his permission to share:

The main memory I have of my experience meditating as a child was the ease with which I could place myself in this space. As we grow up, our stress and anxiety about silence increase, and the practice becomes harder over the years...If you meditate very young, it changes the view you have of the shift to adolescence, and then adulthood: Paying attention to our experiences in the present moment means we watch ourselves as we grow up. Our relationship with the world evolves, and that is the real richness of what I experienced: By looking simply and meditatively at what we're living out, we enter deeply into the complexity of having to grow up and change. Meditation has taught me how "not to give a shit," and now as a teenager, when everything seems increasingly complicated and oppressive, difficult and worrying, this is of real help. If I could give two pieces of advice for instructing children, it would be: First, keep sessions short; children don't need as much time as adults do to find the right position and engage with their experience (I can attest to that!). Second, explain that if it becomes hard for them to meditate a few years later, this is quite normal. I had been warned and so I didn't feel guilty when at thirteen or fourteen, sitting on my cushion suddenly seemed less natural.

CONCLUSION

Reality can only be illuminated by a ray of
poetry. Everything is sleep around us.
　　　　—Georges Braque, *Le Jour et la Nuit*
　　　　　　　　　(*Day and Night*)[1]

For a long time, I was hesitant to talk about the profound happiness that can come from allowing yourself to be. I was afraid this deep, liberating experience would be confused with the limp, watered-down conception of happiness we see in countless magazines and books devoted to well-being.

The act of not giving a shit has nothing to do with this sugar-coated, comfortable happiness. Neither does meditation. Happiness, as I see it, is a genuine adventure, complete with unexpected twists and turns; it can scare us, but it can also make us feel free and alive. We confront its challenges, move past them, and discover uncharted territories. The happiness I refer to is closer to being in awe than to well-being.

It's not an abstract state of constant felicity that nothing can impinge on, but rather the ability to live out a rich and meaningful existence, which, yes, also includes some difficult moments. Suffering is part of it, just as it is part of life. The point is not to waste our time trying to avoid suffering (which is pointless), but to seek to understand it better. For this is how we can begin to lessen, and perhaps even heal it.

If you want to find the wonderment of happiness, the key is to look outside yourself. Open your mind, clear the ground, discover. Allow yourself to be, despite the dominant thoughts that blinker us. To gain a fuller life, you must take risks. Trust life.

Of course, we all have our fears. A few months before his death in 1932, Franz Kafka started to write an extraordinary short story called "The Burrow," which remains unfinished and relatively unknown. The narrator is a half-animal, half-human creature that we know little about, except that it has started building a perfect dwelling to protect it from its invisible enemies. We know nothing about these enemies; we don't have even the slightest clue whether they actually exist. The dwelling is a bunker for the creature to live in, safely separated from the outside world. The creature creates more and more mazes, tunnels, and dead ends; it torments itself thinking up increasingly complex plans and storing up supplies. Its paranoia reaches a crescendo when the dwelling turns into an impregnable fortress. But is it really impregnable? We are this creature, obsessed with building up defense mechanisms that, rather than defending us and supposedly helping us survive, in fact prevent us from living.

Little by little, I allowed myself to marvel at three flowering cherry trees at the bottom of my building, to take the time to look at them, unrecognizable in their springtime blossoming. I felt happy for no reason, or rather for a very great reason: I saw life being reborn and spreading out before me, as in a kind of primordial bounty. "It was like one of those peculiar, poetic, ephemeral, local festivities which people travel long distances to attend on certain fixed occasions, but this one was given by Nature," wrote Marcel Proust, marveling, too, at blooming cherry trees.[2]

I also find myself marveling when I listen to a Mozart concerto, because it teaches me not to be afraid of losing control—because it takes me outside myself. "Whenever I listen to you, I am transported to the threshold of a world which in sunlight or storm, by day and by night, is a good and ordered world. Then, as a human being of the twentieth century, I always find myself blessed with courage (not arrogance), with tempo (not an exaggerated tempo), with purity (not a wearisome purity), with peace (not a slothful peace)," wrote Karl Barth to Mozart, across the centuries.[3] Through music, Barth rediscovered how to trust his intelligence, how to calm down and find a deeper peace, how to trust the vigor of life, that ardent desire that is just waiting for us to get to work.

We have a very mechanical image of our own "internal weather." We assume its barometer depends entirely on external phenomena. That's what we've been told, and we don't raise any objections. And yet, life is far richer than a few passing problems, however troubling they might be. Being audited won't stop us from being happy in other ways, or opening ourselves up to the gifts life continues to offer us.

That said, marveling at the world doesn't mean sheltering ourselves from reality or dreaming with our eyes wide open. It doesn't mean refusing to face up to the difficulties of everyday life and leaving others to deal with them. And it doesn't mean being devoured by such difficulties; it means confronting them while admitting that they are just one part of our lives. It's up to us to search out the other part, by initially recognizing that everything isn't so bad, that we're just experiencing some temporary bullshit. It won't corrupt our entire lives. Even in the worst situations, such amazement is present. Those who accompany people in dire situations, including caretakers for people near the end of their lives, often tell me about the ray of light that appears when they touch the essence of humanity. It emerges from the depths of our being and finally gives us peace.

"To live is so startling, it leaves but little room for other occupations," wrote Emily Dickinson, a poet who means a lot to me.[4] But we're so taken up by other occupations that we forget to exist. We're constantly living out a character: In this case, I'm a mother (or father) and must behave in a given way, I'm a nurse and must act in such a way, or a businessperson who must act like other businesspeople. We're like those masks worn in ancient Greek theater to define the character: a man or a woman, comic or tragic, a human or a god, good or evil. We change masks, hiding behind a front. When am I myself? When do I come in contact with pure life, a thing that cannot be controlled, decided, or mastered, which is always there and at its core can only amaze us? As a prisoner of all my identities, I get the impression that I'm nothing more than my function, my social role, the place I have in my family. By not giving a shit, I rid myself of these functions and turn back into a human being—just a human being. And that is an extraordinary relief.

We can't live constantly in amazement: We're endlessly losing it and needing to seek it out. It cannot be manufactured or invented; all we can do is learn to find it again, to let it appear and rediscover it once more. This isn't about the expert or old person in us, the part of us that claims to understand and wants to analyze everything. This is the inner child in amazement at a ripple in the water, the first poppy in a field, a balloon floating alone in the sky. I know people who have every reason to be happy—they even have perhaps too many—and yet they don't know how to marvel at their good fortune. I know others who, despite their difficulties and problems, keep this spirit alive: They trust in a hope that transcends them, which believers call God, and which I prefer to call our inner treasure.

If I continue to practice, every day (or nearly), it is to continue to be in touch with life. My amazement remains intact, even when things are "bad." I've learned to trust my capacity to be amazed, which makes it so much easier not to give a shit, and experience gratitude—gratitude toward life, toward my own life. Just for being what it is. I admit it took me some time to be able to talk about this amazement I was feeling. Such an approach seemed too watered down, and I was afraid it might override the radicalness that means so much to me, that is to say, the absolute need to stop giving a shit. I now realize this comes down to the same thing: Not giving a shit is nothing other than allowing ourselves to reach this amazement and rediscover that childish spirit we've buried beneath our expertise. Such happiness does not depend on our circumstances, and what a deep deliverance that is.

Appendix

Not giving a shit does not mean giving up. It doesn't mean we quit being committed, or creating, or making an effort. There's some confusion, I know. This stems from a blindness linked to Western thought: We're convinced not giving a shit is the worst thing we could do, that the result would be to sink into passivity and idleness. What a mistake!

I admit it took me several years to see that there is something else between being passive and being active. A vigor we all need to feel more alive.

By "not giving a shit," I mean giving yourself a break. Stop trying so hard to find peace, as if the result were something measurable, like delivering a package or painting a wall. It's something simple to do, and yet it isn't easy. On the contrary! For me, it took a great deal of work over these past thirty years, as can be seen in my previous books (which are more scholarly and technical), before I succeeded in grasping this way of being and experienced its liberating effects.

The first author who helped me along this path was Friedrich Nietzsche. He firmly denounced what is concealed behind our desire to control everything. This desire, he says, is none other than hatred for life. It's what he called nihilism, and what he saw as a threat to our era: the preference for abstract ideas over concrete, everyday experiences. This choice can clearly be seen in our constant use of the verb *to manage* in every possible context. *Managing* does not mean "welcoming," but "planning." It means putting reality into calculable terms. Life becomes a statistical rule. It is not loved but destroyed. The entire project behind Nietzsche's thought was to rediscover life and finally learn to love it.

This requires a surprising move: saying yes to what exists. What Nietzsche called *amor fati*—the love of one's destiny—is what I call "not giving a shit."[1] *Amor fati* has wrongly been assimilated with fatalism, but, as Nietzsche tells us, it doesn't mean giving up, but rather being reconciled with reality. It means it's possible for us to find a new resolve—a creative and happy one.

I've also turned to Heidegger. He helped me understand the profound meaning behind the *confidence* that lies at the heart of the movement I'm inviting you to join—a confidence that challenges many of us. Wanting to be perfect, wanting to be calm, wanting to compare ourselves, and so on (as in the titles of these chapters) are all ways that we lack confidence in ourselves.

The problem comes from the dualistic philosophical conception we have of being human, a conception that leads us seriously astray. We think humans are bodies plus minds, or what philosophers generally call "sensitivity and intelligence." Consequently, we face an irreparable conflict. We separate an imperious sensitivity—our passions, which we judge as foolish—from an intellect that sees only abstractions. We consider the two irreconcilable.

I can never be confident. I am either wrapped up in my sensitivity, or in my intelligence. The only chance I have of finding peace is to sacrifice a part of myself. If I let my intelligence speak, I frustrate my sensitivity. If I let my sensitivity express itself, I bludgeon my intelligence.

In his book *Being and Time* (1927), which set off a shock wave in the history of Western philosophy, Martin Heidegger demonstrated that we are more unified than we think.[2] If I feel happy, then this is no more an experience coming from my understanding than my feelings, no more a bodily experience than an intellectual one. My joy is manifested as much in my gestures and my expressions, as in my thoughts.

The point here is not to go back through Heidegger's complex analyses of what "being" means for humans. "Being," he concludes, means not trying to have total control over yourself and the world—wanting to be perfect, understanding everything, mastering it all—but instead trusting that total openness which is me. The relationship I have with my cup of tea, with the child walking toward me, with the sun coming into the room, is no more intellectual than it is sensitive. It is direct. All I need to do is let it be.

This is what Heidegger called *Gelassenheit*, which is some-times translated as "serenity." And this is what I call "not giving a shit." As Heidegger explained, it means acting in a way which involves both "leaving" and "doing." According to him, this step of trust could liberate our era from the catastrophe threatening us from the fact of wanting to dominate, grasp, and control every-thing.

The philosopher Ludwig Wittgenstein examined this problem from a different angle. He, too, understood the difficulties we have thrown ourselves into, by believing that just our *inner* will can allow us to decide, become involved in, and construct our lives.

But, as he emphasized, when children hurt themselves and cry, they don't convey to their mothers any information acquired through introspection. They express their pain and their moth-ers comfort them.[3] Our minds are not hidden inside us. They run through our behavior. Not giving a shit means dissolving the illusion of an interior confronted with an exterior.

Western thought has been built on the idea that to reconnect with ourselves, we need to cut ourselves off from the world, and separate ourselves from others. How wrong. I can be myself only by opening myself out to the world!

The analysis I have developed in this book, about how teenagers cannot know what they will do later in life, is based on Wittgenstein's thought and his questioning of the myth of a closed inwardness: Teenagers can discover who they are and what they want to do only by being in contact with reality.

This shift has allowed me to understand in what way meditation is a form of openness—an openness to yourself, to others, to the world—and not a kind of introspection, or a sickly self-absorption.

When writing this book, I met many therapists who all explained how their most cutting-edge work involves allowing their patients to give themselves a break, and thus recover their zest for life. This enabled me to gauge the profound effectiveness of the movement I am proposing.

The work of true therapists runs against the idea that it might be possible to rid ourselves of our problems, as if they were old clothes. Telling people who are depressed that they just need to pick themselves up, or someone with dietary problems that it all comes down to a question of willpower, is not only unhelpful, it also creates a lot of guilt.

The psychoanalytic revolution led us to understand that we cannot rid ourselves of the pain of existence. Instead, we can transform it by accepting and living with it. Many of the people who have successfully undergone psychoanalysis say they are the same as before, except that now they are at peace. Thanks to psychoanalysis, they have been able to stop tormenting themselves and can be who they are. The conflict that was stopping them from living has calmed down.

From Carl Jung to Jacques Lacan, the heritage of this approach has led to an ever-finer understanding of this act of abandonment and attentiveness, which is the only one that can free us.

This singular revolution also lies at the heart of Milton Erickson's work, which established the bases of modern hypnosis. Erickson measured the extent to which we are so often prisoners of various fears and limitations. His work focused on undoing the mental patterns that imprison us. Such is the idea of hypnosis: opening a gap in which something new might appear.

Contrary to the popular expression, when there is a problem, there is not always a solution. Often, it is the very idea that there must be solution that stops us from getting better. On the contrary, what we need to do is set ourselves back into our lives.

If my wife leaves me, I lose my job, or have a nervous breakdown, thinking that I need to find the answer prevents me from carrying out the sole work that might soothe me.

Giving ourselves a break is the effect that hypnosis provides: abandoning ourselves totally to the situation we are in. This doesn't mean giving up on the idea of changing, but understanding that change does not come from our will or lack thereof. It is not by deciding that I will no longer be anxious, jealous, or stressed out that I will stop being so. It is only by opening up a space in the situation I've enclosed myself in that I can transform my experience (this idea can also be found in the Palo Alto School of Hypnotherapy).

Meditation in the East also illustrates this very phenomenon. We identify meditation as being an effort to produce a void inside ourselves and reach nirvana. However, the Zen tradition, as founded in twelfth-century Japan by Dogen, is based on the incredible discovery that meditation consists of giving up any form of goal. What I call "not giving a shit" corresponds to the well-known *shikantaza*, or just sitting. You abandon all your projects. You are just there where you are.

In the Tibetan tradition, the path culminates in *Dzogchen*, or the experience of fundamental noneffort. Far from soothing you, any effort to calm yourself down alienates you from your own being. So just be open to who you are, and return to what *Dzogchen* calls your real nature. Don't attempt to stamp out all your troubles to reach some theoretically pleasant elsewhere. Come back to the present. Your own present. This is what is called "touching the bottom," reaching the lowest level of your "being," or "who you are." Not giving a shit means returning to this primordial space. Seeing everything "in terms of openness, space and the inevitable," as Chögyam Trungpa put it.[4]

The same understanding can be found in the West, in Christian contemplation. This practice, which was created by the Greek Desert Fathers, was revived by Teresa of Ávila and John of the Cross in the sixteenth century, then spread throughout seventeenth-century France in an astonishing way, as the doctrine of "pure love." It can be found in the writings of both Madame Guyon[5] and François Fénelon,[6] who emphasize that the whole point is to carry out a gesture of pure giving. Not giving a shit is another name for what Madame Guyon termed "abandonment."[7]

Madame Guyon and Fénelon both thought that the concept of religion as moralizing, ritualized, and guilt-inducing seemed to alienate us from its source. The aim is to love God without expecting anything in return. Without looking for a reward in exchange for our efforts. If I want something at the expense of my love, then I do not really love.

An in-depth study of the founding texts concerning contemplation has allowed me to grasp that giving yourself a break, doing nothing other than being, simply being open to life—or open to God, if you will—is an act of love. Not giving a shit means returning to the often-forgotten source of the most genuine form of love.

My conviction is that these approaches come close to the generally misunderstood teachings of the Buddha and Jesus which, far from being an invitation to a dull religiousness or a simple, conventional morality, are an invitation for us to be fully ourselves, in touch with the root of our own humanity. Both of them showed that far from leading to any form of resignation, only the most complete and radical abandon can give us unrivaled courage and limitless love. What they are inviting us to do is not to give a shit, to accept ourselves more fully, to discover the depths inside us, and thus transform everything.

All of the world's initiatory texts tell us that the fruit of our quest does not lie elsewhere, but inside us. This is the meaning of Homer's *Odyssey*. After his travels through various lands, what Odysseus really wants is to go back home.

Not giving a shit means precisely that: going back home. Not looking for peace and happiness far away—they are right here. If we seek them elsewhere, we will only get lost. Being lost in this way then means always wanting more money, more property, more debt, while never being fulfilled. All the current analyses of contentment, sober happiness, or the need for limitations are based on the intuition that just being here, now, in our being, is the only way that might fulfill us and foster peace in the world.

Such also is the meaning of the myth of Orpheus, whose role in Western history is rather significant. A legendary poet, musician, and prophet in Greek mythology, Orpheus symbolizes the experience of poets who allow poetry to run through them. They don't so much write their texts as receive them. From Pindar in the seventh century BC, to Rainer Maria Rilke in the twentieth century, poets have long meditated on this experience. In one of his most decisive texts, Rilke wrote:

> *Oh Orpheus sings! Oh tall tree in the ear!*
> *And all things hushed. Yet even in that silence*
> *A new beginning, beckoning, change appeared.*[8]

When poetry arrives, it is always the song of Orpheus. And the poet's job is then to create silence in order to listen to this song.

If someone wants to read me a poem, or play me a piece of music, then I have to take a break to tap into a different form of attentiveness. I stop everything—and this can last from a quarter of a second to a few minutes. By giving myself a break, I'm able to arrive at a new way of listening, and a new beginning is possible.

When I was teaching photography at the University of Paris, my students and I used to go to exhibitions by great photographers. The main point was to show them that looking at a picture and appreciating it means allowing yourself to be moved by it and, in a sense, to let it look at you. It means no longer wanting to understand, analyze, reflect.

I've learned a lot from being in contact with artists, poets, musicians, and painters. For them, not giving a shit seems such an obvious move: They say that's where their real talent lies, something no amount of effort could produce. Because no one can decide, through willpower alone, to create a great work of art.

They know how to listen to the voice speaking inside them. They know how to abandon something, to give themselves over to something they can't invent. In reality, the greatest effort an artist can make is to learn how to listen to this gift. The point is: Stop giving a shit.

It is a liberating step, the only one that can release us from the blindness that leads us to mistreat ourselves, destroy the Earth, and along with it our ethical, political sense...

Notes

CHAPTER 1: STOP MEDITATING

1 Translated by Ian Monk.

CHAPTER 2: STOP OBEYING

1 Quoted in James B. Atkinson, introduction to Étienne de La Boétie, *Discourse on Voluntary Servitude*, trans. James B. Atkinson and David Sices, intro. and notes James B. Atkinson (Indianapolis: Hackett Publishing, 2012).

2 Translated by Ian Monk; Marcel Conche, preface to Bernadette Gadomski, *La Boétie, penseur masqué* (Paris: L'Harmattan, 2007). Quotation translated by Ian Monk.

3 Simone Weil, *On the Abolition of All Political Parties*, trans. Simon Leys (New York: New York Review of Books, 2014).

CHAPTER 3: STOP BEING WISE

1 Ludwig Wittgenstein, *Culture and Value*, trans. Peter Winch (Chicago: University of Chicago Press, 1984).

2 Translated by Ian Monk; Georges Thinès and Agnès Lempereur, *Dictionnaire Général des Sciences Humaines*. (Paris: Éditions Universitaires, 1975). Quotation translated by Ian Monk.

3 E. M. Cioran, *The Fall into Time*, trans. Richard Howard (Chicago: Quadrangle, 1970). Page 166.

4 Quoted in Ray Monk, *Ludwig Wittgenstein: The Duty of Genius* (Harmondsworth: Penguin, 1991). Page 91.

5 Marcel Proust, *The Guermantes Way*, trans. Mark Treharne, reprint ed. *In Search of Lost Time*, Vol. 3 (New York: Penguin Classics, 2005). Page 311.

6 Translated by Ian Monk; Charles Baudelaire, "Recueillement," in *Les Fleurs du mal* (1857). Quotation translated by Ian Monk.

7 This story was told by Wangari Maathai, founder of the Green Belt Movement, in "I Will Be a Hummingbird," retrieved from https://www.youtube.com/watch?v=IGMW 6YWjMxw.

CHAPTER 4: STOP BEING CALM

1 Translated from the French by Ian Monk; Marina Tsvétaïéva, *Mon frère féminin: Lettre à l'Amazone* (Paris: Mercure de France, 1989); first published in Russian in 1932. Quotation translated from the French by Ian Monk.

2 Translated by Ian Monk; René Daumal, *L'Évidence absurde* (Essais et notes 1926–1934) (Paris: Gallimard, 1972). Quotation translated by Ian Monk.

3 Kenneth Leach, *True Prayer: An Invitation to Christian Spirituality* (New York: Harper & Row, 1980). Translated by Ian Monk.

CHAPTER 5: STOP HOLDING YOURSELF BACK

1 Quotation translated by Ian Monk.

2 Translated by Ian Monk.

3 Translated by Ian Monk.

4 Mihály Csikszentmihályi, *Flow: The Psychology of Optimal Experience* (New York: Harper & Row, 1990).

CHAPTER 6: STOP BEING PASSIVE

1 Rainer Maria Rilke, *Letters to a Young Poet*, trans. Reginald Snell (New York: Dover, 2002). Page 18.

2 Antoine de Saint-Exupéry, *The Little Prince*, trans. Richard Howard (Boston: Mariner Books/Houghton Mifflin Harcourt, 2000).

3 Antoine de Saint-Exupéry, *The Little Prince*, trans. Richard Howard (Boston: Mariner Books/Houghton Mifflin Harcourt, 2000).

CHAPTER 7: STOP BEING CONSCIOUS

1 Hannah Arendt and Martin Heidegger, *Letters: 1925–1975*, ed. Ursula Ludz, trans. Andrew Shields (Orlando, FL: Harcourt Books, 2004). Page 139.

2 Descartes purportedly used this term while describing a

dream he had, as recorded in Adrien Baillet, *La Vie de Monsieur Descartes* (Paris: Daniel Horthemels, 1691).

3 See Georg Wilhelm Friedrich Hegel, *Phenomenology of Spirit*, trans. A. V. Miller (Oxford: Oxford University Press/Clarendon Press, 1977).

4 See René Descartes, *Discourse on Method and Meditations on First Philosophy*, 4th ed., trans. Donald A. Cress (Indianapolis: Hackett, 1998). Page 35.

5 William Blake, "Auguries of Innocence" in *The Pickering Manuscript* (Whitefish, MT: Kessinger, 2004).

CHAPTER 8: STOP WANTING TO BE PERFECT

1 Translated by Ian Monk; René Char, *Les Matinaux* (Paris: Gallimard, 1969). Quotation translated by Ian Monk.

2 Frank Lewis Dyer and Thomas Commerford Martin, *Edison: His Life and Inventions* (New York: Harper & Brothers, 1910).

3 The show is called *Voix Bouddhistes* in France (and is broadcast on television station France 2).

4 See Anatole France, *The Crime of Sylvestre Bonnard* (1881).

5 Retrieved from http://www.who.int/mediacentre/factsheets/ fs369/en/.

CHAPTER 9: STOP TRYING TO UNDERSTAND EVERYTHING

1 Quotation translated by Ian Monk.

2 Retrieved from http://www.sikorskyarchives.com/IGOR% 20SIKORSKY%20SPEAKS.php.

3 Gerd Gigerenzer and Daniel G. Goldstein, "The Recognition Heuristic: How Ignorance Makes Us Smart," in G. Gigerenzer, P. M. Todd, and the ABC Research Group, *Simple Heuristics That Make Us Smart* (New York: Oxford University Press, 1999).

4 Ludwig Wittgenstein, *Philosophical Investigations*, trans. G. E. M. Anscombe (Malden: Blackwell, 2001 [1953]), quoted in Stanley Cavell, *Philosophy the Day After Tomorrow* (Cambridge, MA: Harvard Belknap Press, 2006). Page 112.

CHAPTER 10: STOP RATIONALIZING

1 Jean Pénard, *Rencontres avec René Char* (Paris: José Corti, 1991). Page 180. Quotation translated by Ian Monk.

2 "France Télécom: Lombard s'excuse pour avoir parlé de 'mode du suicide,'" *Le Monde* (September 16, 2009). Retrieved from http://www.lemonde.fr/la-crise-financiere/article/2009/09/16/lombard-s-excuse-pour-avoir-parle-de-mode-du-suicide_1241095_1101386.html#qoLOZjtp7rz-moiPW.99. Quotation translated by Ian Monk.

CHAPTER 11: STOP COMPARING

1 Quotation translated by Ian Monk.

2 Quotation translated by Ian Monk. See also: Jean-Jacques Rousseau, *Emile, or Treatise on Education*, trans. William H. Payne (Amherst, NY: Prometheus Books, 2003).

3 Georges Bernanos, *Les grands cimetières sous la lune.* (Paris: Le Livre de Poche, 1972). Quotation translated by Ian Monk.

CHAPTER 12: STOP BEING ASHAMED

1 Max Jacob, *Esthétique: Lettres à René Guy Cadou (1937–1944)* (Nantes: Joca Seria, 2001). Quotation translated by Ian Monk.

2 Etty Hillesum, *Het Verstoorde Leven: Dagboek Van Etty Hillesum,* 1941–1943, (Amsterdam: Balans, 2014).

3 Antoine de Saint-Exupéry, *The Little Prince,* trans. Richard Howard (Boston: Mariner Books/Houghton Mifflin Harcourt, 2000).

4 Henry Bauchau, *L'Enfant bleu* (Arles: Actes Sud, 2004). Quotation translated by Ian Monk.

CHAPTER 13: STOP TORMENTING YOURSELF

1 Rainer Maria Rilke, *Letters to a Young Poet,* trans. Reginald Snell (New York: Dover, 2002). Page 39.

2 T. S. Eliot, *The Elder Statesman* (New York: Farrar Straus & Cudahy, 1959).

3 Michel de Montaigne, *The Complete Essays of Montaigne,* trans. Donald M. Frame (Stanford: Stanford University Press, 1958).

4 René Descartes, *Meditations on First Philosophy,* trans. and ed. John Cottingham (Cambridge: Cambridge University Press, 2013). Page 35.

CHAPTER 14: STOP WANTING TO LOVE

1 D. H. Lawrence, "Search for Love," in *The Complete Poems of D. H. Lawrence*, intro. by David Ellis (Hertfordshire, UK: Wordsworth Editions, 1994). Page 552.

CHAPTER 15: STOP DISCIPLINING YOUR KIDS

1 Marcel Proust, *Remembrance of Things Past, Vol. 3: The Captive, The Fugitive & Time Regained,* trans. C. K. Scott Moncrieff and Terence Kilmartin (New York: Vintage Books, 1982). Page 898.

CONCLUSION

1 Translated by Ian Monk.

2 Marcel Proust, *In Search of Lost Time, Vol. 3: The Guermantes Way*, ed. D.J. Enright, trans. S. C. Moncrieff and Terence Kilmartin (New York: Modern Library, 1993). Page 204.

3 Karl Barth, *Wolfgang Amadeus Mozart*, trans. Theologischer Verlag Zurich Clarence K. Pott (Eugene, OR: Wipf & Stock, 2003).

4 Letter to T. W. Higginson, late 1872, in *The Letters of Emily Dickinson*, ed. Thomas H. Johnson (Cambridge: Belknap Press of Harvard University Press, 1986). Page 500.

APPENDIX

1 Friedrich Nietzsche, *The Joyful Wisdom*, trans. Thomas Common (Pantianos Classics, 1910).

2 Martin Heidegger, *Being and Time*, trans. John Macquarrie and Edward Robinson, 7th ed. (New York: Harper Perennial Modern Thought, 2008).

3 Ludwig Wittgenstein, L. *Philosophical Investigations*, ed. G. E. M. Anscombe and R. Rhees, trans. G. E. M. Anscombe, 2nd ed. (Oxford: Blackwell, 2001).

4 Translated by Ian Monk.

5 Jeanne-Marie Bouvier de la Motte-Guyon, commonly known as Madame Guyon (1648–1717), a French mystic, pioneered the set of Christian beliefs known as Quietism, which emphasized the individual's spiritual relationship with God through contemplation and constant prayer. Her book, *A Short and Easy Method of Prayer,* was deemed

heretical by the Roman Catholic Church and resulted in her imprisonment.

6 François de Salignac de la Mothe-Fénelon, or François Fénelon (1651–1715), was a French Roman Catholic archbishop and writer who was influenced by Madame Guyon's ideas. His best-known work, *The Adventures of Telemachus* (1699), is a key work of the eighteenth-century enlightenment in France.

7 See Jeanne Marie Bouvier de La Motte Guyon, *Experiencing Union with God Through Inner Prayer & the Way and Results of Union with God*, trans. Harold J. Chadwick (Orlando, FL: Bridge-Logos, 2001).

8 Rainer Maria Rilke, *Sonnets to Orpheus*, trans. and intro. by David Young (Middletown, CT: Wesleyan University Press, 1987).

Further Reading

The following works are often at my side, and have helped deepen and support my realization that not giving a shit is the key to self-liberation—both personally and collectively.

ON PHILOSOPHY

Fédier, François. *L'art En Liberté: Aristotle, Baudelaire, Proust, Flaubert, Cezanne, Kant, Matisse, Heidegger*. Paris: Pocket, 2006. Print.

Heidegger, Martin. *Contributions to Philosophy (of the Event)*. Trans. Richard Rojcewicz and Daniela Vallega-Neu. Bloomington: Indiana University Press, 2012. Print.

———. *Country Path Conversations*. Trans. Bret W. Davis. Bloomington: Indiana University Press, 2016. Print.

Heidegger, Martin, and Medard Boss. *Zollikon Seminars: Protocols, Conversations, Letters*. Trans. Franz Mayr and Richard Askay. Evanston, IL: Northwestern University Press, 2001. Print.

Weil, Simone. *Simone Weil: An Anthology*. Ed. Siân Miles. London: Penguin, 2005. Print.

Wittgenstein, Ludwig. *Culture and Value: A Selection from the Posthumous Remains*. Ed. G. H. von Wright in collaboration with Heikki

Nyman. Revised edition of the text by Alois Pichler; translated by Peter Winch. Oxford: Blackwell, 1998. Print.

———. *Lectures & Conversations on Aesthetics, Psychology and Religious Belief*. Ed. Cyril Barrett. Malden, MA: Blackwell, 2007. Print.

ON SOCIAL VIOLENCE AND THE COMMODIFICATION OF THE INDIVIDUAL

Diehl, Bruno, and Gerard Doublet. *Orange, Le déchirement: France Télécom ou la dérive du management* (*The Collapse of France Telecom, or the Pitfalls of Management*). Paris: Gallimard, 2010. Print.

Foucault, Michel. *The Essential Foucault: Selections from the Essential Works of Foucault, 1954–1984*. Ed. Paul Rabinow and Nikolas Rose. New York: New Press, 2003. Print.

Legendre, Pierre. *La Fabrique de l'homme Occidental* (*The Fashioning of a Western Man*). Paris: Mille Et Une Nuits, 2000. Print.

Marx, Karl. *Economic and Philosophic Manuscripts of 1844*. Trans. Martin Milligan. Moscow: Progress, 1959. Print.

ON BUDDHISM

Dogen. *Treasury of the True Dharma Eye: Zen Master Dogen's Shobo Genzo*. Trans. Kazuaki Tanahashi. Boston: Shambhala, 2013. Print.

Trungpa, Chögyam. *The Collected Works of Chögyam Trungpa*. Ed. Carolyn Rose Gimian. 8 vols. Boston: Shambhala, 2003. Print.

———. *The Path Is the Goal: A Basic Handbook of Buddhist Meditation*. Ed. Sherab Chödzin. Boston: Shambhala, 2011. Print.

Yixuan. *The Zen Teachings of Master Lin-chi: A Translation of the Lin-chi Lu*. Trans. Burton Watson. New York: Columbia University Press, 1999. Print.

ON CHRISTIAN MYSTICISM

De Caussade, Jean Pierre. *Abandonment to Divine Providence.* Trans. E. J. Strickland. New York: Cosimo Classics, 2007. Print.

Guyon, Jeanne Marie Bouvier de La Motte. *A Short and Easy Method of Prayer.* Trans. Thomas D. Brook. New York: Cosimo Classics, 2007. Print.

Merton, Thomas. *The Inner Experience: Notes on Contemplation.* Ed. William H. Shannon. San Francisco: HarperCollins, 2004. Print.

Piny, Alexandre. *L'oraison du cœur (The Heart's Prayer).* Paris: Cerf, 2013. Print.

ON HYPNOSIS AND THE PALO ALTO SCHOOL OF HYPNOTHERAPY

Erickson, Milton H. *Hypnotic Realities.* New York: Irvington, 1976. Print.

Roustang, François. *Jamais Contre, D'abord: La présence d'un corps.* Paris: Odile Jacob, 2015. Print.

Watzlawick, Paul, John H. Weakland, and Richard Fisch. *Change: Principles of Problem Formation and Problem Resolution.* New York: W. W. Norton, 2011. Print.

ON POSITIVE PSYCHOLOGY

Ben-Shahar, Tal. *Happier: Learn the Secrets to Daily Joy and Lasting Fulfillment.* New York: McGraw-Hill, 2007. Print.

———. *The Pursuit of Perfect: How to Stop Chasing and Start Living a Richer, Happier Life.* Dubuque, IA: McGraw-Hill Contemporary Learning, 2009. Print.

Csikszentmihályi, Mihály. *Flow: The Psychology of Optimal Experience.* New York: Harper Row, 2009. Print.

ON POETRY

Dickinson, Emily. *The Complete Poems of Emily Dickinson*. Ed. Thomas H. Johnson. Boston: Little, Brown, 1960. Print.

Michaux, Henri. *Tent Posts*. Trans. Lynn Hoggard. Los Angeles: Green Integer, 2014. Print.

Rilke, Rainer Maria. *The Poetry of Rilke*. Trans. Edward A. Snow. New York: North Point Press, 2011. Print.

Rilke, Rainer Maria, and Lou Andreas-Salomé. *Rainer Maria Rilke and Lou Andreas-Salomé: The Correspondence*. Trans. Edward A. Snow and Michael Winkler. New York: W. W. Norton, 2006. Print.

Acknowledgments

My thanks to Djénane Kareh Tager, without whom I never would have found a way to say what had been haunting me for so many years.

To Tal Ben-Shahar, for all that we have in common, and for his passion for discovery and knowledge, which has inspired me greatly.

I would also like to express my gratitude to Chögyam Trungpa and his memory: It's been nearly thirty years since I discovered his teachings, and they continue to open my heart. His refutation of any form of exploiting meditation seems more relevant than ever. Access to his work is thanks in large part to the efforts of Carolyn Gimian, who has played a major role in my life.

My thanks as well to Jack Kornfield, Sharon Salzberg, and Karen Armstrong, whom I have the pleasure of publishing in France, and whose work so deeply enriches my teaching. I would also like to thank Léonard Anthony, who accompanied this project with his friendship without ever giving up on what mattered, as well as Susanna Lea, who gracefully opened doors which, without her, would have been too tiring and sad to open.

Thank you to Laura Mamelok, Mark Kessler, Kerry Glencorse, and Cece Ramsey, who support my work as much with their love as with their finesse, intelligence, and precision. They make me a happy author.

My thanks as well to Michelle Howry and the Hachette Books team, to Olivia Morris and her colleagues at Orion, and to Jane Palfreyman and the Allen & Unwin team for all their work.

About the Author

Fabrice Midal has a PhD in philosophy from the University of Paris, is the founder of The Western School of Meditation, and is the author of several bestselling books.